RELIGION AND SCIENTIFIC METHOD

PHILOSOPHICAL STUDIES SERIES
IN PHILOSOPHY

VOLUME 10

GEORGE SCHLESINGER

The University of North Carolina at Chapel Hill

RELIGION AND
SCIENTIFIC METHOD

D. REIDEL PUBLISHING COMPANY

DORDRECHT-HOLLAND / BOSTON-U.S.A.

Library of Congress Cataloging in Publication Data

Schlesinger, G
        Religion and scientific method.

        (Philosophical studies series in philosophy ; v. 10)
        Includes bibliographical references and index.
        1. Theism. 2. Good and evil. 3. Free will
and determinism. 4. Religion and science—
1946—   I. Title.
BL200.S345   210   77—24266
ISBN 90—277—0815—0
ISBN 90—277—0816—9 pbk.

Published by D. Reidel Publishing Company,
P.O. Box 17, Dordrecht, Holland

Sold and distributed in the U.S.A., Canada, and Mexico
by D. Reidel Publishing Company, Inc.
Lincoln Building, 160 Old Derby Street, Hingham,
Mass. 02043, U.S.A.

TABLE OF CONTENTS

PART III

THE CONFIRMATION OF THEISM

ACKNOWLEDGMENTS

I am grateful to the various Editors who permitted me to advance in their journals preliminary versions of a number of ideas here developed with somewhat greater rigor.

INTRODUCTION

I

With the immense success of modern science it has generally become accepted that the only way to acquire knowledge is by the use of the method uniformly practiced by working scientists. Consequently, the credibility of the claims of religion, which seem to be based on belief in revelation, tradition, authority and the like, have been considerably shaken. In the face of the serious threat provided by the ascendancy of modern scientific methodology, religious thinkers have adopted various defensive attitudes. Some have retreated into an extreme position where Theism is completely safe from any attack on it by the use of empirical methods of inquiry, maintaining that contrary to appearances, religion makes no factual claims whatsoever. To be religious, they say, is to subscribe to a certain value system; it is to adopt a set of practices and a given attitude to the meaning and purpose of life without making any assertions about this or that empirical feature of the universe. Others wishing to remain more faithful to what religion traditionally meant throughout the ages, agree that Theism does make factual claims but that these are so radically different from the kind of claims made by science that it is only right that they should be established by a separate method on its own. In matters of faith reliance on widely entrenched tradition and sacred authority is not objectionable according to some. Others have invoked a special kind of experience, accessible only under special circumstances, called religious experience, which they regard as the ultimate foundation on which Theistic claims rest. Yet others have suggested that what is required is a leap of

faith in order to embrace the teaching of religion. Another
interesting way of dealing with the problem is to claim that there
are other very important factual propositions that are inaccessible
to verification through the use of scientific method, such as the
proposition that bodies other than mine also possess a mind and
are not mere robots, and it is universally agreed that it is not
irrational to subscribe to such a proposition. Therefore those who
subscribe to Theism, without establishing it through the use of
scientific method, must not be condemned as irrational either.

While admiring some of the insights achieved through the
various methods of defending Theism just mentioned, I propose to
adopt none of them. First of all I definitely hold that Theism
makes factual claims. In particular it claims that a Perfect Being
exists to whom one may assign at least such properties as
omnipotence and omnibenevolence. I shall also discuss the thesis
that Theism makes factual claims concerning human nature. In
inquiring into the question of the meaningfulness and credibility
of theistic claims no weight will be given to authority, tradition,
religious experience or leaps of faith. I shall treat the proposition
that God exists as one does a scientific hypothesis. I shall examine
the evidence for and against it and its implications, while trying
to uphold the same standards for what counts as adequate evidence or adequate argument that one maintains in a scientific
inquiry. I shall make copious use, mainly in Part II and Part III, of
the most recent results obtained in the philosophy of science.

Now of course it remains true that the classical theistic hypothesis greatly differs from the kind of hypotheses advanced within
science. The latter make claims about some aspects of nature while
the former implies something about all of its aspects; the latter
state that this or that law governs certain phenomena while the
former asserts that all the laws of nature themselves are governed
by God. Yet the question whether all the laws of nature and the
initial conditions are what they are because they just are what
they are without there being anything behind them, or that they

are what they are because of the will of a minded, very intelligent and powerful being seems intelligible in a very straightforward manner, no less than many questions asked by scientists and more so than some questions asked by metaphysicians. It is an important question about the world. There is nothing in the question as such to provide reason for thinking that the observed state of the world cannot be relevant to it. There seem to be grounds for believing that by imposing the generally accepted standards of rigor for arguments supporting the meaningfulness and credibility of putative empirical claims one can make no progress in defending Theism.

II

In Part I of this book I deal with evidence which tends strongly to disconfirm Theism, namely, with the undisputedly observed fact that there is suffering in the world. After trying to explain what exactly the problem, known as the problem of evil, is, I present three viable solutions. The first two are known solutions but I say some things about them that have not been said before. The third is entirely my own. I advanced it first over a decade ago but here are new ways of presenting and defending it.

Part II starts like Part I with the presentation of alleged evidence disconfirming the claims of a great number of Theists, but ends like Part III concluding that the actual evidence at hand may be construed as positively supporting Theism. It deals with the objection based on the views of many scientists that in principle all human choices are predictable, which to many implies a lack of genuine freedom as required by the majority of Theists.

I do not propose to treat exhaustively this topic about which so much has been written (see, for instance, Robert Young's *Freedom, Responsibility and God* (1975) which is entirely devoted to surveying the major arguments associated with this central problem in the philosophy of religion). Rather than discussing known arguments at length I very briefly explain some of the reasons why most traditional believers hold that if it turned out that man was entirely machine-like — in the sense that all his behavior was predictable in principle — and therefore could not be deemed as a responsible, autonomous agent, then the contention that an omnipotent and omnibenevolent being existed would be falsified. In trying to meet this threat to Theism I introduce and consider at length a fairly unfamiliar line of reasoning. At first reading many may feel disposed to be skeptical of what I say. I hope, however, that the reader's final judgement of the soundness of my arguments will not depend on the degree to which they confirm their initial assumptions about the kind of arguments that may be relevant to the topic.[1]

Essentially my thesis is, that given that human beings are free in a minimal and trivial sense, namely, that under some familiar conditions they can act not contrary to how they want to act, it logically follows that some of their acts are in principle unpredictable. Man therefore would have to be looked upon as free in a rather radical sense, for I claim to show that neither a Laplacean demon, nor a parapsychological agent, nor even a divinely inspired prophet could foresee all human choices. Thus the issue of freedom which initially seemed to provide a source of falsification of Theism, is so resolved that matters turn out to be just as required by the hypothesis that God exists. This, on a correct understanding of the notion of confirmation, constitutes a support for the theistic hypothesis.

Most of Part III is devoted to an effort towards clarifying the

---

[1] I also hope that readers will not be put off by what may appear to them as overly technical arguments. Symbols are mainly used since by using them it is possible to repeat a single letter instead of having to use over and over again the same sentence, but otherwise no advanced techniques in any sense are employed. At any rate I should like to urge the reader who feels he can afford no more time to read at least Chapter Fifteen, for it contains the main key to the understanding of Part II.

circumstances under which hypotheses may be said to be confirmable in principle and to the general illumination of the basic nature of scientific method. I have to retravel some of the ground covered in Chapter 2 and 3 of my *Confirmation and Confirmability* (Oxford, 1975), but here I think I have achieved much greater clarity. Upon a correct understanding of the methodology of science, it should become evident that Theism is in principle confirmable by all sorts of possible observations and is in fact confirmed by some actual observations. The meaning of confirmation is to be understood throughout as this: a hypothesis is confirmed by a certain observation if the credibility of the hypothesis in question is higher in the presence of that observation than it would be in its absence.

I should like to point out that we shall not be dealing with any esoteric aspects of science but in fact with very few of its most ubiquitous and basic features only. I shall also not refer to any advanced technical results but merely to some elementary scientific propositions.

III

Two types of potential readers may need some reassurance. First of all there are theists who regard unconditional faith or subjective religious experience as indispensable for supporting the intensity of conviction that is required from a true believer. To them I should like to point out that their position does not demand that they look upon my enterprise as entirely useless, as there is no reason why they should not be interested to find out how Theism fares when treated merely as a hypothesis. My approach does not preclude the ultimate grounding of one's belief upon something loftier than scientific method. It should be remembered that some of the greatest philosophers of the past, who were also deeply religious, thought it important to argue in favour of Theism by using the standards of rationality accepted in their times.

Secondly there are philosophers who no longer regard religion as an important topic to be debated. To those I wish to point out that the greater part of this book is about such secular topics as the nature of infinite regress arguments, personal identity, predictability of human choices, the relation of the past and of the future to the present, the difference between minded men and mindless machines, confirmation and confirmability and the basic nature and justification of scientific method. In fact, apart from the explicit aim to argue for the various theses advanced in this book, there has been the implicit aim to exhibit the richness of the philosophy of religion to show that it impinges upon nearly every important topic in philosophy in general.

PART I

THE PROBLEM OF EVIL

CHAPTER 1

STATING THE PROBLEM OF EVIL

As is well known few of even the best established scientific hypotheses have been or could ever be conclusively proven to be true. While for example we firmly believe that all samples of copper expand when heated, this cannot be conclusively proven true since what we have here is a universal statement referring to an open class, not all of whose members could ever be observed. The widely accepted hypothesis 'Some gases consist of discrete particles', though not a universal statement, nevertheless cannot definitely be shown to be true since it asserts something unobservable. It is only that the hypothesis together with a large number of other hypotheses and assumptions logically implies some true observation statements — statements which are not implied by any other known set of hypotheses and assumptions of comparable adequacy. This confers merely what is called confirmation upon the hypothesis.

However there are some fortunate exceptions. For example, suppose we have formulated a hypothesis H and we know that a given assumption A is true and as a matter of logic H in conjunction with A implies the statement O. Then upon observing that O is false, or that $\sim O$ is true, we have conclusive proof that H is false. This may be put into symbols as has been done by Adolf Grünbaum:[1]

$$[\{(H \& A) \to O\} \& \sim O \& A] \to \sim H$$

which reads: given that H together with A logically implies O *and*

---

[1] *Current Issues in the Philosophy of Science*, Ed. H. Feigl and G. Maxwell (New York, 1961), p. 147. There have been some objections raised against Grünbaum's thesis but these are irrelevant for our purposes.

also that O is false while A is true, *then* it logically follows that
not-H is true.

When it comes to theistic assertions, which are in general further removed from direct observation than scientific assertions,
the situation seems even more beset with uncertainties. However,
quite a large number of thinkers regarded themselves as being in
the happy position of being able to dispose conclusively of theism
by applying the above schema. Let

> H = An omnipotent and omnibenevolent being exists
> (Note: omnipotence includes omniscience),
> A = Benevolence precludes the perpetuating or con-
> doning of suffering,
> O = Suffering does not exist.

Now H & A surely imply that suffering does not exist since God,
who is omnipotent, is powerful enough to prevent it if he does not
want it to exist and he cannot want it to exist since he is omnibenevolent. But suffering exists, that is $\sim$ O is true. A is of course
taken to be true because of the very meaning of the term 'benevolence,' hence [{ (H & A $\rightarrow$ O } & $\sim$ O & A] has been established as
true. Therefore it logically follows that $\sim$ H. In order words, in the
face of all the suffering that goes on in the world, God as conceived by almost all theists cannot be maintained to exist.

Those who want to continue to entertain H must deal with this
problem — known as the problem of evil — before they deal with
anything else. The obvious reason is that there really would not be
much point in considering any of the arguments designed to show
that there are rational grounds upon which to base one's belief in
God, if a solution to the problem of evil was not first found. After
all, what good would it do if we advanced arguments which tend
to support the hypothesis that God exists, if the claim that this
hypothesis was already conclusively refuted remained unchalleng-
ed. It seems therefore clear to me that before we begin to say anything about the considerations that might render the hypothesis

credible, we must attempt to show that we are not trying to establish a falsified and therefore untenable hypothesis.

The strategy that seems to be called for consists in showing that H together with A does not after all imply O. In a well-known paper,[2] Nelson Pike indeed claims what in effect amounts to saying that H and A on their own do not imply O and it is only H & A & A' which logically imply O, where A' = there are no morally sufficient reasons for God to permit suffering. Without trying to suggest what these morally sufficient reasons might be, Pike goes on to say that we cannot be definitely certain that A' is true and thus we no longer have the necessary premisses from which $\sim$ H logically follows.

Pike's point is an important one and we have to assess its relevance to what we have set out to do in this book. Indeed there is a vast number of propositions of which we cannot be certain that we know them to be true and A' is definitely one of them. I believe therefore that Pike has succeeded in blunting the edge of the problem of evil. It can no longer be maintained that there is a logically conclusive proof that $\sim$ H and therefore that God does not exist. Consequently someone with a strong faith in H, may legitimately adhere to his faith even though he is unable (for the time being perhaps only) to suggest why A' is false. Our declared purpose however is to treat H as a hypothesis and consider the question to what extent it may be deemed confirmed by the ordinary standards of scientific method. In the context of our approach Pike's claim will soon be shown very greatly weakened.

To accomplish this we shall compare the situation to the following: suppose in ancient times someone proposes that

$$h = \text{The earth is round.}$$

He may regard his hypothesis confirmed to some extent by such facts as that the lower parts of receding ships always disappear

---

[1] 'Hume on Evil', *Philosophical Review* (1963).

from view before their upper parts. Let it also be given that every-body assumes that

> a = Lunar eclipses are due to the earth's shadow cast upon the moon.

Now it seems that $(h \ \& \ a) \to o$ where

> o = Lunar eclipses are round shaped.

Suppose however that it had always been observed that the shape of lunar eclipses was rectangular. This would give us

$$[\{(h \ \& \ a) \to o \} \ \& \sim o \ \& \ a]$$

which logically implies that $\sim h$, i.e., the earth is not round. Imagine now that our scientist can think of nothing better in order to save his hypothesis than to point out that it is not strictly the case that $(h \ \& \ a) \to o$, it is only that $(h \ \& \ a \ \& \ a') \to o$ where

> a' = Under no circumstances do round objects cast rectangular shadows.

But he goes on to argue that it is by no means absolutely certain that a' is true, hence the proof that $\sim h$, i.e., that the earth is not round, fails.

The correct reply to this is quite obvious. Indeed, in spite of having observed rectangular lunar eclipses only, there would be no absolute proof that $\sim h$, however, it would strongly be confirmed that $\sim h$. In general, round objects have never been known to cast rectangular shadows; our scientist offers no plausible explanation why in the case of the earth this might be different. Unless he comes forward with a reasonable specific suggestion why the earth might be in a different category than other opaque objects, it is rational to maintain that $\sim o$ provides strong empirical sup-port that $\sim h$.

The situation in our case does not seem so different. In general, permitting suffering is incompatible with benevolence. The morally sufficient excuse that one could think of, is that all the suffering permitted by God is necessary for achieving some noble purpose, which he, though omnipotent, could not otherwise achieve. As long as a plausible specific suggestion is not made as to what this purpose might be, $\sim$ H, i.e., the atheistic hypothesis, seems strongly supported empirically.

In this book we are specifically precluded from availing ourselves of the kind of argument offered by Pike. For when we come to considering the positive arguments in favor of theism in Part III, I shall not permit the resisting of such arguments by objecting to them that although admittedly it seems at the moment that certain facts are best explained by the theistic hypothesis, we cannot be absolutely certain that after all there is no better explanation. The atheist cannot, as I shall have opportunity to elaborate later, appeal to the possibility of good explanations the specific nature of which he cannot spell out. Obviously I cannot have it both ways; when confronted with the problems of evil, the theist must not be permitted this either.

At any rate everyone will agree that if some plausible specific explanation is offered as to why A' is false, rather than just making the logically correct point that we do know for certain that A' is true, the theist will be in a much better position. At this stage it seems to me that the situation is the following: while it has not been conclusively proven that the theistic hypothesis is false it has come under serious attack. It is not merely that the theistic hypothesis seems to lack positive support which would lead merely to agnosticism: there appears to be strong *prima facia* evidence that it is false and thus atheism seems supported.

CHAPTER 2

THE IRRELEVANCE OF THE AMOUNT OF EVIL

In an attempt to shed more light on our topic let me stress that while the question of the amount of evil the world contains most vitally affects our lives, in the context of our problem this is an entirely irrelevant question. Some defenders of theism have tacitly assumed the contrary to be the case. Some have movingly urged that we acknowledge the great abundance of goodness in the world. Instead of focusing attention on the things we lack, we ought to show appreciation for the fact that the important things in life are free. We ungrateful humans tend to overlook that the essentials of life are available most of the time for most of the people. However, not only in real life do we seem to hold that good news is no news, but even in literature it is mostly the bad which is highlighted. There are very few significant novels about people whose needs are supplied and lives are fulfilled; literature thrives on anguish and misery, defeat and tragedy. Sinful as we are, we keep complaining about what we do not like, regarding it as unfair that we should be subjected to any deprivation, while passing over all the support and benefit received, regarding all of it as ours by right. An unbiased observer should however realize that the amount of good in the world by far outstrips the amount of bad. A man of faith ought to go even further, denying that there is any real evil in the world, believing that all suffering is instrumental in eventually bringing about a great amount of benefits to both the sufferer and others.

Now there may be much truth in this. We are indeed by nature creatures who are rarely enraptured by the fact that there is nearly always enough air to breathe, water to drink and firm ground to stand on, that many parts of our bodies are so marvellously constructed as to adapt themselves to an ever changing environment and to perform extraordinarily complex tasks; but we are easily aroused to deplore hardships when they occur. But none of this has any bearing on our problem. It may well be that there is really much more to rejoice about than to bemoan. It may even be that often, or if you like, always, suffering turns out to have been merely an unpleasant way of bringing about a greater benefit of such a high degree that the sufferer himself, had be been aware of the benefit, would have agreed that it was worthwhile enduring his bitter experiences. None of this affects our problem in the least. Had we been dealing with someone less than omnipotent who was supposed to be running the universe, such considerations would have been relevant: after all, he is doing remarkably well, he should be applauded. But in the context of an omnipotent being such considerations carry no weight for we are entitled to expect absolute perfection and the slightest distress, even if it eventually leads to great improvements, is intolerable. It would not make any difference if instead of what we have now, everyone's life was a continual bliss, except that a single individual had to endure a slight inconvenience for a brief moment and that even this turned out to be instrumental in bringing about great benefit to himself and others. The problem would of course not be felt so acutely or would not be noticed at all, but logically it would exist no less than it exists now. In a perfect world, it seems that nobody should be allowed to suffer at all, and an Omnipotent Being should be able to bring about everything that is desirable in a way that does not inconvenience anyone.

It is well to remember that this point about the irrelevance of the amount of suffering that goes on, to the problem at hand, works in the other direction as well. Some people think that there is too much evil in the world. They would be quite prepared to put up with a certain amount of misery but find the existing amount excessive. There are thinkers who hold that some of the events of the twentieth century render it impossible that an omnipotent, omnibenevolent ruler of the universe exists. Richard R. Rubinstein is one of those who maintains this. At one place he declared:

After Auschwitz many Jews did not need Nietzsche to tell them that the old God of Jewish patriarchal monotheism was dead beyond all hope of resurrection.[1]

Another theologian, Eugene B. Borowitz, also refers to people who take this attitude:

Any God who could permit the Holocaust, who could remain silent during it, who could 'hide His face' while it dragged on, was not worth believing in. There might well be a limit to how much we could understand about Him, but Auschwitz demanded an unreasonable suspension of understanding. In the face of such great evil, God, the good and the powerful, was too inexplicable, so men said 'God is dead'.[2]

Thus to some people, apparently, while the atrocities perpetuated in previous centuries were still reconcilable with a belief in a loving God those of our own age were no longer so.

Now it is probably true that the horrors of Nazism are quite unprecedented in history not only in scope but even in quality, and it will be long before we shall gain an understanding as to how human beings are capable of doing what the Nazis did. However, the advent of the German concentration camps has not in any way augmented the problem of evil. There is a logical incompatibility among omnipotence, omnibenevolence and the existence of evil, and this incompatibility is quite independent of the quantity and quality of evil. If, on the other hand, a way can be found of showing that human suffering does not necessarily constitute evil, then again the problem disappears irrespective of the amount of suffering that goes on. Thus either a belief in God was impossible ever since the beginning of the human race and its attendant miseries, or it is still possible in our own days. I know of no

---

[1] *After Auschwitz* (The Bobbs Merrill Company, 1966), p. 227.
[2] *The Mask Jews Wear* (New York, 1973), p. 199.

plausible attempt to solve the problem of evil which permits the existence of all human suffering that went on prior to World War II, but is unable to accommodate the suffering which occurred thereafter.

CHAPTER 3

THE STANDARD BY WHICH
DIVINE ACTS ARE APPRAISED

The most natural attempt to answer the question as to how it is that a benevolent God does to people what among human beings would strongly be condemned as evil is to say that God does not have the same obligations toward his creatures as his creatures have toward one another. If I cause unnecessary suffering to my fellow man that is evil, for he and I are on the same level of creation, he is a completely autonomous being *vis-à-vis* me, whose person I must regard as sacrosanct at all times. But God, to whom we all owe our existence and without whose constant supervision and help we could not be sustained for a single moment, can take liberties with us which we are forbidden to take with each other.

Let me emphasize that this attempt must be sharply distinguished from the attempt of denying that the term 'good' has the same meaning when applied to God as when applied to human beings. Such a solution to the problem of evil was already ruled out by John Stuart Mill who declared:

'I will call no being good who is not what I mean when I apply that epithet to my fellow creatures; and if such a being can sentence me to hell for not so calling him, to hell I will go.'[1]

Of course not everybody would be as unyielding as Mill and be prepared to suffer in hell rather than give up a philosophical point. Most of us would surrender to superior force and call God good if he insisted on it, but of course the word would be emptied of its meaning. In the same way, we would be prepared to call him green to save ourselves. 'Green' of course means 'has a surface which

[1] *An Examination of Sir William Hamilton's Philosophy* (Longman, Green & Co., 1865), p. 129.

reflects green light only', and God has no surface at all; so by calling God green we would be merely using a word by which we meant nothing. Thus God could not be regarded any more omnibenevolent than he could be regarded omnigreen, since benevolence has also a fixed meaning, namely, not causing unnecessary suffering to humans. And if we do not mean this then we are applying an empty term to God. It will not help to say that 'good' as applied to God need not remain undefined since we can define it by saying that 'good' is 'whatever God does'. This still would not render the assignment of goodness to God any more significant than the assignment of greenness, even though 'Divine greenness' might be defined as 'the color God has'.

But the approach which I shall propose, and which is more plausible, does not deny that the same standards apply when we assess the actions of God as when we assess our own actions, nor that the meaning of 'good' is exactly the same whether applied to God or humans, however radically God's circumstances differ from ours. Some say we too, if there existed beings to whom we stood in the relationship in which God stands to us, would be allowed the same liberties God is allowed to take toward us; and God too, if there were a being with whom he stood in hierarchical equality, as we do with our fellow humans, would be restricted *vis-à-vis* him, the way we are. James F. Ross, for example, goes so far as to claim that God's relationship to his creatures may be compared to an author's relationship to his fictitious characters, the creatures of his imagination.[2] According to him just as Shakespeare is not to be blamed for allowing King Lear to suffer so much, God is not blameworthy for not preventing his creatures from suffering. Not many would be prepared to go along with this, simply because we, even though mere creatures, are nevertheless real, whereas characters of fiction are not. This however does not matter. We may very well admit that there just do not happen to be beings who stand

[2] *Introduction to the Philosophy of Religion* (London, 1969), pp. 135–48.

to us as we stand to God. This is no way invalidates the claim that even though we do not change our standards of morality when we assess Divine actions toward us, we can nevertheless not evaluate them in the way we evaluate human behavior in the existing context, but rather in the way humans would have to behave toward creatures who were completely dependent on them and owe everything to them, had there been such creatures.

But what we must ask is, is God's relation to us so greatly different from our relations to each other that he is devoid of all moral obligations, and no constraints whatever apply to his actions? If the answer is yes then indeed it is impossible to attribute any evil to God, but neither does it seem possible to attribute any goodness to him. After all a man who is morally permitted to do anything he likes to his typewriter and who is therefore not in the least blameworthy for illtreating it, is not to be regarded as behaving in a morally commendable way no matter how kind he is to his typewriter.

Perhaps it might seem that one could nevertheless assign goodness to God by virtue of the fact that the counterfactual 'Had God had any peers, he would never have caused them any suffering' was true. But this is untenable. First of all it cannot be consistently stated that there be more than one omnipotent being, and it is seriously to be doubted whether a counterfactual the antecedent of which was logically false is meaningful at all. Does it make sense to say "Had the number nine been the number eight it would have been even"? Secondly we must ask, on what basis do we claim this counterfactual to be true? The truth of it manifests itself in no way since there is nothing in the actions of God relevant to it. The most, it seems, that one could say in its support, is that it must be true that if God had any peers he would never cause them any suffering since he is good, which is plainly circular. Lastly, and perhaps more decisively, the claim that we may assign goodness to God on the basis of the assertability of this counterfactual fails because it is an essential part of theistic belief that God is good to *us.* Even if the counterfactual could be shown to be meaningful and true, it would in no way imply that God was good to human beings.

We cannot therefore maintain that our complete dependence on God renders it entirely irrelevant what he does to us. We stand in relation to him, it might be said, neither like the typewriter stands to its owner nor like King Lear stands to Shakespeare. We are, after all, real sentient beings. Consequently, while he is not at all obliged to refrain from causing us suffering, if he nevertheless goes out of his way, so to speak, to prevent us from a lot of suffering we could have been made to endure, and bestows upon us a great deal of benefits, which he undeniably does, then this amounts to goodness on his part. The fact that he has no obligations whatsoever toward us does not lessen but on the contrary enhances his goodness: there are no restrictions as to the amount of suffering to which he is permitted to subject us, yet he restricts himself, making us suffer just so much and no more; he is not obliged to grant us any benefits, yet he volunteers to give us plenty.

But this defense will not do either. If we say that God's refraining from subjecting us to more suffering represents goodness on his part, then if he refrained even more that would amount to an even higher degree of goodness. To be omnibenevolent would require that he should refrain to a maximum degree from causing any suffering, that is, cause no suffering at all. Thus, while on this version of what relationship between us and God our complete dependence upon him implies, unlike on the previous version, he could be called good; yet he could nevertheless not be called all good.

CHAPTER 4

SUFFERING AS PUNISHMENT

I shall begin my defense of theism by citing a most readily available solution which goes back to antiquity, one of which everybody has heard. This solution has however fallen into general disfavor and there are rarely any theodicies nowadays which make reference to it. Later I shall try to suggest some reasons which may be responsible for the fact that this solution has these days been nearly universally ignored.

The solution to which I am referring is that all suffering is Divine punishment for sins. God is omnipotent and omnibenevolent but evil does not exist, since there is no unnecessary suffering; for people suffer because of the necessity to expiate their sins.

Some may find this unacceptable because they are altogether opposed to punishment as such. Among humans, they may approve of measures to be taken against criminals, but these measures may be justified only because they tend to prevent further crime, as when a criminal is incarcerated and is thus isolated from the community which he can no longer harm; or at most these measures may be justified as a deterrent which will discourage the person punished from sinning again, and also will influence others to refrain from wrong-doing out of fear of reprisal. But they deny that criminals actually *deserve* punishment and refuse to allow punishment for its own sake, punishment as retribution. Consequently in God's case there can be no justification for punishment at all. Surely if God does not desire that certain deeds be performed then he, being omnipotent, can find more pleasant ways of preventing such deeds than bringing down painful punishment upon sinners. Thus the only ground for Divine punishment there might be is retribution, which is unjustifiable.

Against this attempt to invalidate the present solution I have to point out a general rule which applies to all solutions to the problem of evil. When it is argued that God is justified in conducting the world in the way he does we may be attributing to him a certain value judgement. It may happen that the value judgement we have to attribute to God differs from the one to which we would readily subscribe. We cannot insist that God's value judgements coincide exactly with ours. What we may insist upon is that they be not absurd. But if a certain solution to the problem of evil implies that God holds a view about values which has been held by some people whom we regard as otherwise fairly enlightened, then even if we do not happen to subscribe to this view we must not therefore reject the solution. The view that punishment is justified as retribution even among humans has been held by some thoughtful people, and some arguments have been produced for this view which cannot be ruled out as entirely absurd. The claim that all suffering is due to defying the will of God can therefore not be rejected out of hand.

Before going on to consider what has seemed to many the most devastating objection to the present attempt to solve the problem of evil, let me discuss the interesting claim that it would have been much kinder on the part of God if he did not allow anyone to sin. Justice may require that sin be punished, however, let there be no sin and there will be no need for punishment. To this one will want to reply that God wishes to have a world in which creatures who can exercise their free will exist. Human free will is such a precious quality that it is better to have a world in which this quality can be manifested, even though people will inevitably sin and have to suffer, than to have a world in which there is no suffering at all because people are prevented from sinning at the cost of their freedom.

An objector can, however, persist by saying that the best of all possible worlds is one in which both desirable states of affairs prevail, namely that freewill is present and suffering is absent, and that such a world is possible. God's failure to bring about such a world is evidence that he is not omnibenevolent. The argument that such a world was possible runs as follows: there are people who never (or almost never) sin. We admire such people. The fact that we admire them shows that we do not believe that saintly people have no freewill. It is universally believed that saints are not people who are incapable of sinning but people who are subject to the same strong temptations as everybody else but who freely exercise great restraint and manage always to do the right thing. When God is about to create a given individual, he in his omniscience knows whether that individual is going to lead a righteous or a wicked life. If he foresees that the individual is going to be a sinner, he should not allow him to be born. In this way he would ensure that the world was inhabited by saints only, who would not bring any punishment upon themselves, and we could have a world in which free will was preserved yet no one suffered.

To answer this objection, it might be sufficient, to claim that those people who are not completely righteous and hence have to suffer for their transgressions are better off existing than not existing. They themselves, when in the world to come — assuming now without comment that such a world exists — they review their earthly lives which contained much unhappiness but which also provided them with the opportunity to earn through their acts of freewill the great bliss in which they now partake, will conclude that, in spite of the suffering they brought upon themselves through sin, it was much better to have gone all through that than not to have been born at all. God in his omniscience does indeed foresee what any creature endowed with free will is going to do, yet his omnibenevolence does not imply that he allows no one to be born who is not assured to lead a sin-free life. A world in which no sinners are permitted to exist is not the best of all possible worlds. The existence of some sinners, i.e., those who are not as exceedingly sinful as to bring upon themselves retribution of such magnitude that they would be better off not existing, improves the world.

At this point some readers may think they have a number of obvious objections. One of them runs as follows: perhaps most people lead lives that are valuable in spite of the amount of unhappiness they contain. But surely there have been also people whose lives have been so exceedingly wretched and filled with horror that they themselves have dearly wished never to have been born.

This objection at once disappears if one assumes the few decades of a man's single earthly life span represent a negligible fraction of his total existence, which stretches into the far-beyond, from whence even the most misery filled physical life may seem well compensated for.

A somewhat better objection would be the following: perhaps most people are sinful, but on the balance their virtuous acts outnumber or outweigh their transgressions and therefore earn more reward then punishment. But surely there have also been people who had led thoroughly wicked lives; their crimes by far outweighing whatever good they have done. Such religiously and morally corrupt people earn far more punishment than reward for the duration of their whole existence. For these people, even from the vantage point of eternity, it would have been better never to have been born. How does one explain the existence of a Hilter or a Stalin? God would have been kinder to *them* by not allowing them ever to have come into existence.

This objection assumes that all the acts of the notoriously wicked are acts of free will and therefore inevitably draw upon their perpetrators Divine retribution. But this would be very difficult to show to be the case. Sometimes a sinner may simply be the scourge of God who is forced to act the way he does in order to further a Divine plan. Pharaoh, who, in spite of the plagues, continued in his refusal to let the Hebrew slaves go, may not have done so against his will — he wanted to continue to enslave them

— but he *had* to want to do so. We are told, after all, that at a certain stage God had 'hardened his heart' and forced him to go on in his sinful ways since it fulfilled the Divine purpose of the occasion. We are to presume that Pharaoh was punished only for those of his vicious acts which he performed in the period before he lost his freewill. It could therefore be claimed that there never has existed anyone whose freely willed acts contained so much evil as to necessitate an excessive amount of punishment rendering his existence less valuable than his nonexistence.

I shall not examine any further these or other objections, since the whole problem of why God does not create only people with free will of whom he knows that they are to lead a completely virtuous life, assumes that it is logically possible to have an agent possessing freewill and foresee all his acts. This has however been denied for widely different arguments which include those of Gersonides[1] and Plantinga.[2] I shall not defend or repeat their arguments but present one of my own in Part II. In fact the main purpose of Part II is to develop as carefully and as clearly as I can an argument to show that it is logically impossible to predict at least some freely willed choices. But if it is logically impossible to create a person, some of whose actions are freely willed, and at the same time foresee exactly what he will do, then even God cannot perform such a task. As is well known, and as I shall also explain in the next section, God cannot do, and is not required to do, what it is logically impossible for him to do. He cannot therefore make sure that he brings into existence only such free agents who will lead blameless lives. But to have a world which is inhabited by agents whose acts include genuinely free acts which may bring forth punishment is preferable to having a world free of suffering, but also devoid of human free will.

[1] Levi ben Gersom, *The Commentary of Levi ben Gersom (Gersonides) on the Book of Job* (New York, 1946), p. 50.
[2] Alvin Plantinga, *God and Other Minds* (Cornell, 1967), pp. 168–73.

CHAPTER 5

THE QUESTION OF AN AFTERLIFE

I

In this chapter I propose to devote some discussion to what has been regarded as the most damaging objection to the present solution, namely that there does not seem to be any correlation between sinfulness and suffering. There are people who are universally acknowledged as pious and kind, yet whose lives are a series of misfortunes, while others who are obviously wicked, lead prosperous, long lives. It is of course well known that many theists believe that the life of a person upon this earth is an infinitesimally small part of his total life, which continues in the thereafter where the balance is redressed. Perfection is very rare, and perfectly evil people exist no more than perfectly saintly people. Hence wicked people deserve some reward and pious people some punishment. All that is required is that, on the whole, pious people should be much better off than wicked ones, and this, given an afterlife, God can easily ensure. However the point is that many philosophers find such an answer entirely unacceptable.

Another objection points at the suffering of innocent children who cannot be held responsible for anything they do. The answer that these may be suffering for sins of their parents can legitimately be claimed to be based on an absurd and therefore unacceptable value judgement, namely, that it is right to punish one person for the sins of another. The sufferings of children can, however, be explained on an assumption which some find even much more objectionable than the disembodied survival of death, namely the transmigration of souls. On this assumption, a newly born baby may be the reincarnation of a person who had lived earlier and who may be punished for his past misdeeds in his present life.

I should like to dwell for a while on this highly discredited notion of the transmigration of souls. It is not my intention to support the credibility of the claim that some person X may be the reincarnation of Y, only to inquire into the question: must one be regarded as utterly deranged if one maintains the possibility that this claim may be true?

The reason why a serious philosopher might want to declare the notion of the transmigration of souls as nonsense is that he may claim it as incoherent, being based on an incoherent notion of personal identity. Personal identity is ensured either by memory or bodily continuity. The newborn child neither remembers anything of his previous existence nor is his body continuous with the body of the person whose continuation he is supposed to be. He cannot therefore be identical with a departed person.

This claim however does not stand on unshakeable foundations. In the next three sections of this chapter I should like to sketch the outlines of a view of personal identity which denies that memory or bodily continuity play any important role in determining personal identity. Many books have been written on the subject of personal identity. To put forward in a fully convincing manner a highly unorthodox new view on the matter, such as mine, would require much more space than I can afford here. What I do hope to achieve, however, through my brief sketch, is that the reader will agree that this view deserves to be further explored or at least that it deserves a hearing.

II

Suppose we perform an operation on A's skull and excise that part of his brain which houses all his memories and transplant this memory bank into the head of B. It is then conceivable that B should acquire several millions of new memory items by virtue of having A's memory bank connected to his nervous system without acquiring all the memories of A. To be more specific, any skill A had, any information or the memory of any physical event having happened that A possessed, has been transferred to B's memory store, however B remembers no emotion of feeling A has experienced or in general no mental event that occurred to A. In particular if A has seen, heard or felt that S is P, then B will not be able to recall having actually perceived S to be P — i.e., he will have no retrospective memory of the matter, to use Furlong's term — he will only remember *that* S is P.

The most reasonable explanation in such a situation seems to be that B is capable now of possessing an item of information or a specific skill which he would have been capable of obtaining himself in the first place had he himself been trained to acquire that skill in the past or been given the information in question earlier. Thus, for example, if A's memory file contained an item of memory that a physical event P has taken place at time t, then B now remembers that P has occurred at t since it is possible, in principle, that at t, B should have been witnessing P happening. But a mental event M_A, that is a mental event which takes place in the mind of A, can feature only in the experience of A; B cannot live through experiencing M_A in the first place and, consequently, he is incapable of having such an experience recorded in his memory. B is capable of remembering any physical event A is capable of remembering; but when it comes to mental events, he can remember only events of the type M_B, that is mental events which he can experience at the time when they are occurring. But of course A does not and could not possess in his memory any event of the kind M_B; thus there are no mental events which he possesses that could be transplanted into the memory store of B.

Under these circumstances it would seem reasonable to conclude that A cannot be regarded as essentially the person who possesses a given brain, since the brain associated with A has been superplanted onto B's brain, without the latter acquiring A's personhood. Also if m is the set of the millions of memory items transferred from A to B, A cannot be said to be essentially the person who possesses m since if that were so B would have now become A and there would be no reason why he could not after all be capable of remembering M_A. It would still remain true however that personal identity and memory content are intimately related. But rather than saying that the question whether a person is A or B is dependent on what memories he possesses we would have to say that it was the other way round. Given that a person is who he is, he is capable of recalling the kind of experiences which he could have lived through in the first place.

Therefore, in the light of the results of our brain surgery, the following position concerning personal identity would seem reasonable. B is who he is by virtue of the specific mind he possesses, a mind which can be associated with different brains and bodies as well as all sorts of experiences and memories. When it comes however to inner experiences there is an important limitation on the kind B may partake of. The experiences must be of mental events which occur in the mental world of B. Events occurring in the mental world of another person are entirely out of B's reach. It is therefore, in principle, impossible to create in B's memory the remembrance of an A-type mental event which only person A, but not he, might have experienced. There is, of course, no reason why we should not create for B — who never in fact had a toothache before — the memory of having had a toothache of exactly the duration, intensity and quality A had experienced. But of course B then would remember that he, B, had a toothache, that is he would have a mental trace of a kind of event which took place in his mental universe, which is a fundamentally different remembered experience than the toothache A had, which occurred in the mental universe of A.

The B-ness of B consists in there being a unique mental universe which constitute B's mind and in the ability to experience any event at all which takes place in this universe. The B-ness of B specifically does not consist of him having a given body or a certain set of memories. Also, we may vary the life history of B in unlimited fashion without thereby interfering with the B-ness of B. That is, B's mental universe may be filled with an unlimited variety of different events, but of necessity of events which occur in that universe and not events occurring in another's mental universe. Also, when it comes to the memory of mental events, B can have an unrestricted variety of them except that they must be memories of events having occurred in B's mental world. It is quite understandable then why if all the memories of A are transplanted into the mind of B, in place of M_A there is now a blank: the memory of M_A itself, which has occurred in an alien mental world, cannot be implanted on B's mind. You could of course create a corresponding event M_B in B's mind, which is an exactly similar event to M_A except that it occurs in B's mental world, and therefore experiencing it is not beyond the range of B's mind. But we are not now manufacturing new memories, we are merely transferring those which exist in A's memory bank, and there is no M_B to transfer from A to B.

I have been considering the question of what theory of personal identity might be the most reasonable to hold if certain empirical discoveries were made. Such discoveries of course have not in fact been made. But since they must be admitted as in principle possible, the theory just expounded must even now be conceded as a legitimate theory to subscribe to.

III

The previous point may be approached from another angle as well. It was Wittgenstein who said that it is logically possible for me to feel pain in someone else's body. Let us dwell for a moment on this assertion. Not everyone is ready to concede at once that it must obviously be true. It is best therefore to explain in stages why it is indeed undeniably true that I could, in principle, feel pain in, say, Smith's arm. I can feel pain in my own arm. Now

suppose my arm is severed from my body so that no nerve from
my arm leads to my brain for there is a very narrow air gap between my arm and my body. Nobody would deny that it is still
logically possible for me to continue to feel pain in my arm since
logic certainly does not require that neural transmission cannot
take place across an air gap. We can now gradually increase this
gap. At no stage does it make sense to suddenly insist that it is no
longer logically possible to continue to feel pain in my arm. Now
we may cut off Smith's arm and sew on my arm onto his body in
its place, which should not logically interfere with the situation
either. But it surely makes no difference if the arm at present
connected to Smith's shoulder was originally connected to me or
was always a part of his body; in both cases I should, in principle,
be able to feel pain in it.

Accepting then that I can feel pain in Smith's arm, we may ask
how do I identify a given pain in Smith's arm as my pain. It
would certainly seem that I employ no specific criterion in my
identification but, in fact, what I do is identify the pain as mine
directly, not via anything else. It would definitely not be correct
to say that I identify a given pain as mine through the fact that it
occurs in my body. Apart from all the other reasons against saying
this we now also have the argument that in the case before us, for
example, the pain in question is not located in my body and yet I
know at once that it is mine. In fact, I do not have to perform any
particular act of identification in order to secure this knowledge.
When I happen to be in pain I become immediately aware that I
am in pain. But given that I am in pain, there is no question to be
settled as to whose pain I feel. It is a necessary truth that I can feel
only my own pain. So the fact that a given pain exists as well as
the fact that it belongs to me is given to me at once.

Thus concerning the problem of personal identity this much
will probably be conceded by all: Suppose it is asked, given that a
person feels a particular pain p_1 at t_1 and also that a person feels
p_2 at t_2, how do we ascertain whether it is the same person who is

in pain at these two times? When the answer to this question is sought by people who are not those who feel pain p_1 and p_2, then there is indeed a problem of whether to use this or that criterion of identification. But in the case of the person who feels p_1 and p_2 there is no problem; he may dispense with all criteria. He becomes aware at once, directly at t_1 that he has p_1 and at t_2 that he has p_2. Given to him this, that is, given that it is *he* who has had p_1 as well as p_2 it is also given to him at once that it is the same person who has p_1 and p_2. However, what some philosophers might still insist upon is that it is an entirely different question to ask, by virtue of what unifying feature both p_1 and p_2 possess, is it a fact that they belong to the same person? And when it comes to this question of ontology, rather than that of knowledge by the subject, the only answer that could be correct may seem: by virtue of the fact that they are both causally connected to the same body. But now we can see that this answer must be wrong. After all, the pain in the case under consideration is causally connected with Smith's body and not with mine, yet it belongs to me as well as do other pains which are causally connected with my body. Thus causal connection with one and the same body is neither a necessary condition for belonging to the same person, since I can feel the pain which is located in Smith's body: nor is it a sufficient condition, since Smith does not feel that same pain even though it is located in his own body.

What then is the correct answer to the question: by virtue of what unifying factor do p_1 and p_2 belong to the same individual? I believe that it is by virtue of the fact that p_1 and p_2 occur in the same mental world or are experienced by the same mind. This however may at once seem to create a problem. The sameness of a given mind we are now told is not determined by it being associated with a particular body. Nor is the identity of a given mind determined by the unique kind of experiences associated with it since, as already indicated, A's mind may partake in exactly similar experiences as that of B, except that A's experiences consist of

mental events occurring in A's mental world, unlike B's experiences that are mental events which take place in B's mental world.
But surely we cannot simply uphold the empty claim that A's
mind is essentially the mind which belongs to A whereas B's mind
is different in that it belongs to B. We must be able to point to
some concrete feature which distinguishes A's mind from B's, and
hence A from B.

A brief possible solution to this problem might be sketched
thus: Imagine two persons X and Y; to X every colored surface
looks red and to Y every colored surface looks green. Suppose
there is a trapezoid-shaped colored surface in the visual field of
both X and Y. Then X and Y may be said to have exactly similar
color-vision experiences, to the utmost degree of similarity to
which they are capable of having such experiences. Thus while
both X and Y have the experience of seeing a trapezoid-shaped
colored figure of the same size and situated at the same spot, their
experiences are not merely numerically different, but have also an
important, unbridgeable qualitative difference between them. X's
color-vision experience is different from Y's and the former cannot even imagine the specific quality of the experience the latter
is having. Conversely also, if, of two persons X and Y, it is said that
one of them has the experience of seeing a red surface, we at once
know it must be X. In other words, as soon as we are given the
specific quality of the color-vision that is being experienced we
know the mind with which it is associated; the specific quality of
an experience determines the mind which experiences it.

Something like this could be the case in general. When A experiences a certain pain of a specific detailed description and B has a
pain experience of exactly the same description, then it may very
well be the case that the two pain experiences are not merely
numerically distinct but have also some basic qualitative difference
between them. In other words, while the pain experienced by A is
exactly similar to the one experienced by B in every respect as far
as intersubjective description can go, they are essentially different

just as the color-vision experiences of X and Y are different. In fact, given that a pain has a distinctive A-quality it follows that A is the only person who is capable of experiencing it. Thus it could be maintained that the A-ness of A is independent of the body or the bodies with which he is associated and also that A is capable of being the subject of an unrestricted variety of experiences and memories. Even before A has had any experiences at all, his unique identity was determined by the specific kind of experiences he was *capable* of experiencing. All experiences, pleasant or unpleasant, must be of a specific flavor before A can experience them, and if they have this specific flavor then no other mind can partake of them.

IV

In the famous *Analysis* competition series in the fifties one of the questions posed was 'How can one wish to have been Napoleon?'

It is remarkable that all the three authors of the winning entries as well apparently, as Strawson, who set the question, assumed it as obvious that in a straightforward sense the wish was incoherent. What the competitors did, therefore, was to discuss either the question of how to treat logically incoherent wishes or how to provide the wish with some plausible reinterpretation according to which one does not literally wish to have been Napoleon but something else which makes sense and try to find out what this something else might be. It seems that the wish to be Napoleon was treated as in the same category as my wish that the chair beside me were a crocodile. This latter wish, if taken literally, is certainly incoherent. I may well wish that the chair turned into a crocodile, which would strictly mean that on the spot where the chair now stands there is no chair and its place is occupied by a crocodile. But if the wish were fulfilled it would just not be true that the chair itself was the crocodile. For once we have a full blown crocodile we no longer have a chair at all, and it is the crocodile which is the crocodile and not the chair. Similarly it is Napoleon who is Napoleon whereas I am I; it is possible for me to be a fluent speaker of French and I may even become a general or the emperor of France but not Napoleon himself. I could also, of course, cease to exist or never have existed at all, but I could not turn into Napoleon or have been Napoleon; for it is always Napoleon, and no one else, who is Napoleon.

In the light of what has been said before however, there does not seem to be any difficulty for me to literally wish to be Napoleon. I could (logically) certainly have his body without ceasing to be me, since a change of body does not necessarily affect my identity. But, of course, I am wishing something much more fargoing, namely that all the events that happened to Napoleon should have happened to me. I would, of course, then not end up with having experiences identical with those which were had by Napoleon, only with experiences that are similar to the maximum degree to which two experiences that are had by two different minds may be similar. I would thus completely change places with Napoleon with respect to all the physical aspects that are part of his life history but still retain my own mind. Therefore the mental events which occurred to me would, after all, be basically different from those which occurred to him in as much as they would have been the type of events which only my mind, and no one else's mind, is capable of experiencing. Also of course, my memories would be of mental events that occurred in my mental world and not in the mind that has actually happened to be associated with Napoleon.

To the outside world nothing would seem to have happened if the desired change did actually take place. No feature of the world, to which anyone except myself and the mind now associated with Napoleon has access, would be different, if I were Napoleon. In the present circumstances I know that I possess a certain body in the sense that I feel pain in it, and it obeys my will that is different from that of Napoleon. If my wish were fulfilled then I would be aware that I feel pain in what is commonly known as Napoleon's body, which would also obey my will – and also that all the extraordinary deeds performed by Napoleon were performed by me. But since the body and the deeds in question would look no different from what they look now, no one would be aware of any change.

The situation with the chair and the crocodile is very different. After the chair becomes the crocodile, supposedly nothing of its previous 'chair'-hood is left, for otherwise it would not have become a genuine full fledged crocodile. But when I become Napoleon, that means that all the physical properties, processes and events associated with Napoleon would be associated with me but I would fully retain my own mind. Thus, while my external life would be most fundamentally different, I would continue to be able to experience the same kinds of mental events I am capable of experiencing now and which can occur in no one else's mental world.

Bernard Williams, who has also written about the issue discussed here, argues that anyone who regards the wish to be Napoleon as a coherent wish must hold the belief that I could remain I even after shedding all my individuating properties.[1] He holds this position because he thinks that if I changed body with Napoleon, assuming fully his role while not having any of the experiences that are my present lot, then I would discard all the characteristics that are constitutive of me being the person who I am and would retain none of my individuating properties. To continue to regard me as me even after I have ceased to have any of my distinguishing features is to uphold the view that the self is some mysterious extra entity that exists apart from one's body, history and characteristics, something immutable, basic and also indescribable. His attitude is, of course, correct on the assumptions that the identity of a mind is determined by the experiences it partakes in.

[1] Bernard Williams, *Problems of the Self* (Cambridge, 1973), p.41.

The position espoused here however is that the same mind can partake of an unrestricted variety of experiences. The identity of a given mind is determined by the unique quality the experiences need to have in order that it should be capable of partaking of them. Thus, without being given my body or any of the mental events associated with me, I have the unique individuating property which consists in the specific type of experience I have a potential to undergo.

I wish it were 1954 now (another wish which I take to be coherent) and I could submit my entry to the *Analysis* competition. In it I would argue that not only does it makes sense for me to wish to have been Napoleon but also, if what I have said is correct, then it makes sense to claim that it is in principle possible that I could actually have been Napoleon: for I might be a reincarnation of him, his mind now being associated with this body of mine.

V

Apart from anything said in the last three sections it should also be pointed out that the coherence of the claim that a living person X may be identical with a departed person Y, may be defended by subscribing to a view concerning identity which is very similar to the one accounting for personal identity in terms of bodily continuity. Two persons are identical if they have the same body. But sameness of body is not determined by continuity; it is ensured by having the same uniquely distinguishing characteristics. It is assumed that every particular body has a large set of characteristics which is unique to it. Fingerprints are believed to be one such characteristic, but there might be indefinitely many, especially on the microscopic level. The new-born baby may then be said to be the reincarnation of a person long dead by virtue of his having all the unique bodily characteristics possessed by that person. This view is not without its difficulties. It may not, in fact, ever have happened that two contemporaneous bodies share the same characterizing properties, but this is logically possible, in which case we would be faced with the absurdity of having to maintain that two contemporaneous separate bodies were numerically identical. This however is a difficulty which philosophers who regard the body as the core of a person do *anyhow* have to face. It is, after all, conceivable that two separate bodies should evolve continuously from one and the same body.

The reader should also be reminded that a vast number of volumes have been written defending the view according to which the identity of a person is ensured by his having the same immutable spiritual substance commonly referred to as the soul. Some theists firmly believe that the soul constitutes the essential core of a person who can shed and assume different bodies and set of memories. The coherence of the notion of 'soul' if defended can, of course, secure the coherence of the notion of 'transmigration of soul' as well as disembodied existence. But after having defended, in the previous three sections, the coherence of the claim that a person is not to be identified with his body or set of memories, I shall not further defend any views supporting the present solution.

The point really is that there are people who simply do not wish to hear arguments about this matter. Whether or not they find the claim that there is life after death too abhorrent to contemplate, they will not only refuse to be informed about any alleged evidence in support of this claim[2] but will dismiss it as inherently absurd with no desire to argue their case.

Let me illustrate. John Hick in his book,[3] in trying to answer the oft raised objection to the theistic world view that it is meaningless since unverifiable, says that it may be verifiable in the

---

[2] e.g., The investigations conducted by Kubler-Ross of the reports of patients who had been pronounced dead and consequently recovered. Cf. *Newsweek*, July 12, 1976.

[3] *Faith and Knowledge* (Cornell, 1957) pp. 150–62.

after life where both believer and unbeliever will verify to themselves through a more direct confrontation with the Divine, that the theistic doctrines were correct. Now let me emphasize that I happen to believe that Hick's suggestion is not necessary: for as I shall explain in Part III, on a correct understanding of the nature of empirical verification or confirmation, the significance of theism may be claimed to be assured to be significant by its being verifiable in the here and now. Nevertheless Hick's contention cannot be dismissed out of hand. To say that, no, the theistic world view is not verifiable since there is no afterlife is obviously to beg the question. One could conceivably contend that the verification principle requires that all significant statements be rooted in possible experiences in this life, a contention which once again could only be well secured by insisting that after all these are the only experiences. Yet a reviewer[4] of Hick's book has this to say:

...he is driven into making use of the bizarre device of eschatological verification to save the day: we shall see when we die who is right, the naturalist or the theist. But what could experience after death possibly contribute that experience now cannot. The dead cannot be epistemically any better off than we are.

But surely one could go on and depict endlessly many logically possible experiences in the afterlife which would make it at least as difficult to deny the hypothesis that God exists as it is now difficult to deny the hypothesis that electrons exist (which I take to be verified). But I do not think that Kennick was interested in hearing about this since he felt that the whole device of eschatological verification was bizarre, for reasons he did not think it necessary to elaborate. I believe an impartial reader — which of course is a very rare specimen indeed in matters of religion — should judge Kennick as unduly hasty in his condemnation of Hick.

[4] W. E. Kennick, *Philosophical Review* 57 (1958), p. 409.

Still it is a fact that in the Old Testament, for example, no explicit mention is made of an afterlife, which may be an indication that it is desirable for a believer to be able to work out a scheme of things which also makes sense in the context of the here and now alone. The next solution to the problem of evil I am about to discuss makes only very peripheral use of the notion of an afterlife; and in the last solution merely a brief mention in passing is made to the whole notion.

CHAPTER 6

THE 'SOUL MAKING' THEODICY

Before continuing with any attempt to solve our problem, let me emphasize one point, the lack of appreciation of which has put many people in an unreceptive frame of mind toward what might be quite legitimate solutions to the problem of evil. One must sharply distinguish between what amounts to a logically sound reply to the challenge that the theist is faced with, the inconsistent triad 'God is omnipotent', 'God is omnibenevolent' and 'Evil exists' and what may constitute an effective way to console a sufferer. There are suggestions which do one and not the other. When it is convincingly pointed out to a grief stricken person that things may not be as bad as they seem, that his suffering is valuable in enriching his life by deepening his understanding of good and evil, or in ultimately bringing about other benefits to himself and others, this may alleviate his pain and 'solve' the problem that is troubling him but has no effect whatever on blunting the acuteness of the logical problem of evil. On the other hand a solution based on abstract but sound arguments showing that an omnibenevolent being need not do away with all suffering, is logically effective in combatting the claim that consistency demands the denial of the existence of God, but not at all effective in comforting a mourner. The two solutions to be proposed are, I believe, of such a nature. They constitute no suitable answers, for example, to the question of a bereaved person as to why he had to sustain such a loss. In fact, it would be callous to quote any solutions of their kind as an answer to his cry. But we must not allow ourselves to be influenced into thinking that this detracts from the soundness of these answers to the question to which they are addressed.

Both solutions presuppose that an omnipotent being is unable to do what is logically impossible for him to do. There are few things in the world about which all philosophers agree, but this may be one of the things about which the highest proportion of philosophers agree: it does not detract from God's power if he is unable to perform tasks that are logically impossible for him to do. The reason for this seems quite simple. A being is omnipotent as long as there is no task which he is unable to perform. If God were not omnipotent there would have to be a task which he could not perform. True enough God can, for example, not name the highest integer. But it is logically impossible to name the highest integer since there is no such thing. Thus God's failure to perform the 'task' of naming the highest integer is not a failure to perform a task since there is just no such task as naming the highest integer.

The solution I want to introduce in this section has been discussed at great length by, among others, John Hick who has called it the 'Soul Making' theodicy and has provided forceful exposition of it in several of his works. This solution is based on the claim that there are certain very valuable human qualities, the possibility of which God could not have ensured without permitting suffering. Consider such noble human characteristics as fortitude, charity, compassion or forgiveness. It is logically impossible to have instances of the exercise of fortitude when there is no pain since by definition fortitude is the courage to bear pain; it is logically impossible to have charity when there is no want, compassion when there is nothing to be compassionate about, or forgiveness when no injury has been done. A world which contains instances in which these desirable qualities are manifested through appropriate acts is a better world than one in which they are not. God, wanting to have a better world, had to allow suffering.

The first and obvious objection to this will be that the reason we admire virtuous responses to suffering is because they are instrumental in alleviating it. In the absence of suffering these responses have no value of their own; their value lies solely in their effectiveness to mitigate pain. Thus, in a world in which there was no pain, there would be no need for these responses, which would therefore lose all their usefulness. It is absurd, so it might be claimed, to create pain so as to render certain human acts possible, the sole aim of which is the overcoming of pain.

The answer to this, however, is that the view according to which the value of the noble characteristics here referred to, lies solely in their effectiveness as antidotes to suffering, and hence varies directly with the amount of suffering there is, is a possible view. But there is also another view which is by no means absurd, according to which these characteristics constitute good in themselves. One way of defending this view is to point out that a person who has exercised charity, for example, has done good, not only because he has eliminated want, but because he has enhanced his character by being charitable. Admittedly, if the want did not exist we would not need the act of charity to eliminate it, but we would be missing out on a chance to improve the character of the giver. Charitable people are valuable, not merely because they are useful, but because they possess noble characters. The theist claims that it is this second view which he ascribes to God, who is therefore justified in creating suffering which can bring forth virtuous responses whose function is not merely to mitigate or eliminate suffering, but also to increase the virtues of those who so respond.

I have heard it asked 'But surely this solution does not require that all the great variety of suffering, which calls forth different kinds of virtuous responses from a large number of people, should actually exist. It would be sufficient that we merely *sincerely believed* that it existed'. But, of course, we may then ask the objector how does he *know* that it really exists and that he is not merely made to believe that it does, by being presented with genuinely convincing evidence that there is a lot of suffering in the world? He may conceivably complain 'But I know with certainty that my own sufferings are real', to which of course, we may reply that they have to be for otherwise he would not believe that others are actually suffering either.

Some people have also been worried by the question: what about the sufferer himself? Is it fair to him that he be made to endure pain for the possible spiritual benefit to others? The 'Soul Making' theodicist may reply to this that God's responsibility to be fair is not merely to this or that individual but to the world as a whole, which he has to ensure is the best of all possible worlds. A world devoid of suffering and also of the possibility for virtuous response to suffering, is inferior to a world in which both existed. Thus he created the latter.

It may also be pointed out that the defenders of this solution could claim that it goes back as far as the Bible. Although the intimate connection between behavior and the attendant reward and punishment is continually stressed there, it is explicitly written that the sufferings of Job were not due to any wrong-doings on his part. The standard interpretation is that he was tormented for the sake of spiritual enrichment, mainly to provide him with an opportunity to actively display his immense fortitude and put into practice his tenacious conviction in the ultimate justice of the Lord in the face of most adverse evidence. Incidentally − as mentioned in Job, Chapter 42 v. 11 − an opportunity was also provided for 'all his brothers and sisters and all who had known him before' to show sympathy and comfort him. Then in the next verse it says 'And the Lord blessed the latter days of Job more than his beginning', indicating that he was abundantly compensated for the ordeal he had gone through. In the last verse of the book we are told 'And Job died. . .full of days', the Hebrew expression for which is usually understood to mean 'fully satisfied'. Thus we may take it that in the end Job had no complaints. It may perhaps be presumed that ultimately he fully understood the higher purpose of his sufferings and conse-quently he himself deemed them as justified. This, of course, does not happen to most sufferers. Many defenders of the 'Soul Making' theodicy may, however, believe in an afterlife where a person could be compensated for the pains he had to undergo in this life and even assent to their worthwhileness.

CHAPTER 7

THE QUESTION OF MORAL EVIL

The attempt to solve the problem of evil in the way just expounded has been subjected to an ingenious attack by J. L. Mackie. In an article often referred to,[1] he points out that if we are to assume that charity, compassion and so on are such desirable qualities, it is worthwhile having earthquakes, hurricanes and all sorts of dreadful diseases just for the sake of securing their existence, then cruelty, meanness and the like are of a comparable degree of undesirability. Just as we have said that the man who responds virtuously to suffering does far more good than just lessening the amount of suffering in the world — for he also enhances his moral character — so we would have to agree that a man who responds callously to suffering does much more evil than just leaving suffering to continue, which he could have alleviated, by debasing his own character. If it is claimed that God has greatly improved the world by providing opportunities for virtuous responses to suffering to exist, then it would also have to be admitted that he has impaired the world to no less degree by also providing opportunities for vicious responses. Surely the world could have been no worse off by having opportunities for neither.

To put it slightly differently: the world contains first order good and evil. First order goods are food, shelter, good health and the like. First order evils are lack of food, shelter, good health and so on. The justification for the existence of first order evils was that they make it possible that there be second order goods, which in essence are human qualities associated with the efforts to eliminate first order evils. But the world also contains second

---

[1] 'Evil and Omnipotence', *Mind* (1955), pp. 200–12.

order evils, which are base human qualities associated with the efforts to perpetuate evil and the need of having second order good does not explain that.

A possible way out of this difficulty is to suggest that the existence of second order evil is justified by the need of having a yet higher order good, third order goods, which are human qualities associated with efforts to curb those who are trying to perpetuate first order evil. Third order good is triply good, for it tends to diminish the amount of first order and second order evil as well as enhance the character of its practitioner. The existence of third order good is important enough to justify the existence of second order evil without which it could not exist. But then the question arises as to why there is also third order evil, which in turn is explained by the need for fourth order good, and so on, leading us to an infinite regress.

Mackie goes only as far as to say that the defense according to which the existence of evil is justified, because of the virtuous responses it may provoke, is involved in a regress, without examining the question whether the regress is a vicious one. But, in fact, it seems that here we face a very peculiar regress, and it is by no means clear that it is a vicious regress. Admittedly, one can look at the regress in a way which suggests that we cannot escape our difficulties, since as soon as we have justified the existence of evil of level $n - 1$ by pointing out that it is a necessary precondition for the existence of good of level n, the question arises as to how we justify evil of level n. Thus, every attempt to solve the problem is frustrated once we realize that there is evil of the same level as the good, the existence of which was so important to secure. But there is also a way of looking at matters which suggests that all our difficulties disappear. For as soon as the question is raised why do we have evil of level n, we are able to explain this as a necessary prerequisite for having good of level $n + 1$. It is not clear why we have to look at matters pessimistically and emphasize that after every solution we are immediately confronted with a new problem and not optimistically, emphasizing that for every question raised we are at once provided with a solution.

Mackie has constructed a peculiar kind of regress in which we alternate between a step which lands us in a difficulty and a step which resolves that difficulty, and it would seem that something further has to be said before it is clear that, because of this regress, the proposed solution to the problem of evil fails. Clearly, when a philosopher wants to invalidate an argument by claiming that it gives rise to a regress, the onus is on him to show that the regress is vicious. How would Mackie do this?

Mackie's regress is not entirely unique; its kind has been considered before. We find it in connection with McTaggart's famous argument for the unreality of time. McTaggart points out that the statements 'E is in the future', 'E is in the present' and 'E is in the past' are incompatible statements, yet they are true of the same event E. To remove the contradiction it will be said that these statements which are indeed incompatible when asserted at the same time, may all be truly asserted at different times. 'E is in the future' is true if asserted at M_1, a moment which precedes E; while 'E is in the present' is true if asserted at a later time M_2 at which E occurs; and 'E is in the past' is true if asserted at yet a later time M_3. This indeed removes the problem we found concerning the incompatible statements which are true of E, but what about statements we may assert about M_1 for example? It seems that three incompatible statements, similar to the statements made about E_1 can be formulated referring to M_1 i.e., 'M_1 is in the future' etc. The answer of course is that these difficulties too can be eliminated in the way we eliminated the difficulties concerning E: the incompatible statements are true only if asserted at different times; that is, 'M_1 is in the future' is true when asserted at M_4 before M_1 and so on. But then difficulties arise concerning statements about M_4 and so on *ad infinitum*. No matter how many difficulties we solve new ones can always be generated. This raises an infinite regress as a result of which McTaggart claims that we must abandon the view that properties, like being in the future, in the present or in the past, are real properties of events or dates.

Arthur Prior raises what seems to be essentially the objection I have raised against Mackie:

Even if we are somehow compelled to move forward in this way [i.e., taking further and further steps along the regress] we only get contradictions half the time, and it is not obvious why we should regard these rather than their running mates as the correct stopping points.[2]

Prior's position is that a regress is clearly vicious only if one cannot rest at any stage along it without being involved in a difficulty; however, in the case of McTaggart, only if we stop at an odd step along the regress, but not if we stop at an even step, do we have a contradiction. The way to defend McTaggart is to show[3] that, if we stop at an even step, then we are involved in another kind of difficulty equally unacceptable to him, and this forces us to move on to an odd step where we face a contradiction. If McTaggart is right that at every step along we are involved in some kind of a difficulty which Prior did not take into account, then his regress is vicious, since we cannot come to rest at an even step because of one kind of difficulty nor at an odd step because of another. Similarly, here in order to establish definitely the viciousness of his regress, Mackie would have to show that the theist cannot rest at a stage where he explains the existence of nth level evil by its providing an opportunity for $n + 1th$ level good because of some difficulty and has to move on to the next step, where we have also $n + 1th$ level evil, which is left unexplained.

But one may perhaps attempt to defend Mackie by insisting that infinite levels of good and evil are merely conceptual possibilities, but that, in fact, we do not have orders of good and evil beyond a certain level. It is quite absurd to think, for example, that in prac-

---

[2] *Past, Present, and Future*, p. 5.
[3] G. Schlesinger, 'The Structure of McTaggart's Argument', *The Review of Metaphysics* (June, 1971), p. 675.

tice there is good of level 537, which is associated with the attempt to stop those who are trying to combat those who are endeavoring to curb those and so on 537 times, who practice charity. We may find in the world third order good, perhaps even fifth order good, but it surely cannot go much higher. Where this stops in practice there is an empirical question which would be exceedingly difficult to answer, but it is very reasonable to assume that, if the highest level of good practices in this world is n, then so is the highest level of bad. But then, of course, the problem of evil remains.

To this, however, the theist may reply that he is prepared to admit that, in practice, there is a limit to the level of good and evil that exist and that he too does not know how far these levels go; however, he believes that God in his goodness, if he allowed good of level n to exist, did not permit the existence of evil of an order higher than $n - 1$ level.

We must not, of course, fail to mention that to this question, as to why moral evil — which is what second and higher order evils are — is permitted to exist in the world, a large number of philosophers have adopted a different approach. They have applied what has become known as the 'free will defense'. God regards the existence of agents with free will as of overriding importance, but such agents will, from time to time, choose to do what is evil. The question why does he then not create free agents, of whom he is assured that they will do no wrong, has been considered in Chapter 4 and will be further discussed in Part II of this book. To form some impression of the central importance for the problem of evil that the 'free will defence' has recently assumed, the reader may for example consult the writings of Antony Flew,[4] Alvin Plantinga,[5] Clement Dore[6] and Stephen Davis.[7]

---

[4] 'Divine Omnipotence and Human Freedom' in *New Essays in Philosophical Theology*, ed. A. Flew and A. MacIntyre (London, 1955).
[5] *God and Other Minds* (Ithaca, N. Y., 1967).
[6] 'Plantinga on the Free Will Defence' *Review of Metaphysics* (1971).
[7] *American Philosophical Quarterly* (1970), pp. 119–30.

CHAPTER 8

THE JUSTIFICATION
FOR CREATING OPPORTUNITIES
FOR VIRTUOUS RESPONSE

Clement Dore, in his important article 'An examination of the "Soul Making" Theodicy', discusses at length some other objections to the solution to the problem of evil under review. One objection is that while we have explained the existence of suffering, which is redeemed by the virtuous responses it provokes, what about those sufferings nobody responds virtuously to? He claims that the world contains many instances of apparently useless suffering, that is, suffering which is not instrumental in bringing about noble actions or noble states of mind and that we require an explanation as to why God has allowed these to occur. Throughout his discussion he seems to assume that God does know beforehand how agents possessing free will are going to react in any given situation.

In his answer, Dore considers the question: how would the world have to differ from ours in order to satisfy us that it might be governed by an omnibenevolent being. After considering the various alternatives he concludes that it cannot be proved that any world different from ours would be a better world and hence an omnibenevolent being was permitted to create a world like ours. The first alternative world he calls W_1. In W_1 whenever I choose not to take any action to alleviate it, God abolishes the suffering. It is clear however, Dore maintains, that W_1, in spite of the fact that it would contain much less suffering than our world, would not be a better world. In our world when I alleviate pain I am doing something truly good, for in the absence of my action the suffering would continue, in W_1 however, my charitable and compassionate acts have no moral significance: the suffering they are designed to alleviate would cease anyhow.

Next he considers W_2 in which whenever God in his omniscience knows that if a certain instance of suffering were to occur then I would choose not to react virtuously to it, he then prevents the suffering from ever occurring in the first place. In W_2 it is no longer the case that it is pointless for me to take any counteraction to suffering since the distress which I mitigate is mitigated only because of my action — it would not disappear by itself. Still Dore claims that W_2 would not be a better world than ours, since virtuous acts are only truly good if they are freely chosen. For in W_2, when I take action designed to relieve someone's suffering, it is false that I could have on that very occasion chosen not to do so, since if God had known that I would make this latter choice, he would have removed the opportunity for me to make it by never having permitted the suffering to take place.

Not everybody would be happy to grant Dore his view of free will. When there are no physical factors constraining my actions and I do exactly what I want, then just because in some sense of the word 'could' I could not act differently, since if I were to act differently then the opportunity for so acting would not have arisen in the first place, then it is not indisputably clear that I lack free will. Also it would seem that one might ask the question why the world is not like W_2' which is slightly different from W_2 in that in W_2', whenever God in his omniscience knows that if a certain instance of suffering were to occur *everybody* would choose not to react virtuously to it, he then prevents the suffering from occurring in the first place. In W_2' even Dore would have no grounds for claiming that my virtuous responses are not freely chosen since it is no longer the case that if God had known that I would choose not to react virtuously to a given instance of suffering, he would have removed the opportunity for me to make such a choice by never permitting the suffering to occur in the first place. He might have permitted it, since somebody else will respond virtuously to it. It may seem, perhaps, that W_2' has the disadvantage of W_1 in that there is no point in my counteracting suffering which will anyhow be relieved by somebody. But while it is sure that if I choose to do nothing about your suffering someone *eventually* will relieve it, there is still much value in my acting now and relieving it earlier.

From what Dore says in connection with another question, it seems however, that he would maintain that W_2 is not a better world than ours. The value of a virtuous act varies with what would happen in its absence. If it is the case that if I do not act to relieve your suffering then it will not be relieved by anyone, then my act is more valuable than if it is the case that even if I do not act someone will eventually act to relieve it.

Granting the validity of everything Dore claims, it still seems that he has provided an answer only for why there should be cases of suffering with respect to which I and everybody choose not to respond virtuously. But there is no explanation for why there should also be cases where an instance of suffering fails to evoke any virtuous response, not because everybody chooses not to respond virtuously, but because there is no opportunity for anyone to choose an attitude toward it. Consider, for example, a child who, in an abandoned house, locks himself into an old refrigerator and suffocates to death. His plight provides no scope for any choice to be made as to how to respond to it. The child himself is not yet of the age when he can react with fortitude to his own suffering and others have no opportunity to respond or not to respond virtuously, since the child's predicament is not known to anyone at the time and is only inferred later when, long after his death, someone opens the refrigerator. Nothing that Dore says in his paper explains why such instances of suffering are permitted to occur. So, while Dore may have shown that an omnibenevolent being could create a world in which, when I am confronted with an instance of suffering with respect to which I choose not to react virtuously that suffering may continue indefinitely so as to lend greater value to my acts on those occasions in which I choose to react virtuously, it is not explained why he can also create a world in which suffering not confronted by any morally responsible beings occurs.

The answer, however, it seems to me, is that cases of suffering which are, in principle, unknowable to anyone either at the time of their occurrence or at any later time cannot, for obvious reasons, be claimed to be known to exist. Any instance of suffering, of which we are certain that it passed unnoticed, must at least be known after it has passed, otherwise it would not be known that it took place. But those people who eventually learn that an instance of suffering had taken place, even if they cannot do anything to affect it, nevertheless have the opportunity to respond virtuously to it by regretting it and deploring it. To be sorry and compassionate about someone else's suffering, even if it has already passed and nothing can be done to alleviate it, is still a noble act which enhances the character of the person who harbors such sentiments. Also, a person is strongly aroused by the human tragedies of the past, may preserve and nurture the benevolent spirit thus generated in him, which may inform all his consequent acts of altruism. But once we realize that an instance of suffering may be justified by the virtuous responses it evokes, not necessarily at the time when something can still be done to alleviate it, but at any time, Dore's problem does not arise in the first place. One simply cannot have evidence that useless suffering, i.e., suffering which never has and never will evoke virtuous response from anyone, has ever occurred.

A very important and initially most disturbing question which is also discussed by Dore is the following: A human being who claims that he should not be condemned for causing unnecessary suffering, since by his acts he has created the opportunity for others to respond virtuously, would certainly not be exonerated. Our refusal ever to condone among humans the causing of unnecessary suffering shows that we subscribe to the view that it is better not to have any opportunities for virtuous responses and no suffering than to have both. Then it ought to be true, also, that if God prevented all the suffering in the world it would be come a better place than it is now.

This question can, I believe, be formulated even more sharply. It is not merely a fact that in our society we would resolutely reject a criminal's excuse that in injuring his victim he has provided opportunities for virtuous responses, it seems necessary that we should reject such an excuse. Suppose I cause A unnecessary suffering, but in order to render my act morally defensible, I point out that I have provided B with the opportunity for creating higher order good by counteracting the effects of my deed and healing the wounds I have caused. But why is B's healing those wounds to be regarded as commendable? After all, by doing so he removes the opportunity for C to respond virtuously to the presence of these wounds. If B is callous and instead of healing those wounds he sprinkles salt on them, he would not only have provided opportunity for others to heal even more severe wounds, but also to fight B and thus enhance their moral status through fighting an evil-doer. But if thus we refrain from attributing any value to B's actions in healing the wounds A has caused, then A providing B with the opportunity to perform them, cannot be regarded as doing any good either.

It seems to me, however, that there are a number of ways in which to meet this objection. First of all, one can say that a human being is never justified in creating evil of any order and of any amount, since neither can he forecast well enough what the responses of other free agents will be nor can he estimate correctly how much the disvalue of evil of one kind is offset by the value introduced through securing the possibility of a given amount of good. God on the other hand, even if the view expounded in the next chapter is accepted, according to which he may not know with certainty what an entirely free willed reaction of a human being is going to be, can, as will be explained, gauge with complete accuracy what the probability of every possible reaction is. Also, he, having a perfectly accurate scale of values, knows how much good of what kind compensates for what amount and kind of evil. We can claim, therefore, that whenever God allows suffering to occur he knows, or at least estimates, that it is highly probable that it will evoke virtuous responses of sufficient degree and amount.

A second and perhaps more fundamental way of meeting this objection, is by pointing out that it does not merely happen to be a fact that in our society we would resolutely reject a criminal's excuse that in injuring his victim he has provided opportunities for virtuous responses, but that we are compelled to reject such an excuse. Suppose this was not so. Then A may inflict unnecessary suffering upon his victim; but in order to render his act morally defensible, he points out that he has provided B with the opportunity for creating higher order good by counteracting the effects of A's deed and healing the wounds he has caused. But why is B's healing those wounds to be regarded as commendable? After all, by doing so he removes the opportunity for C to respond virtuously to the presence of these wounds and to the behavior of A and B. But then C might be judged praisworthy if he further aggravated the victim's wound for the benefit of D and so on. This may be carried on indefinitely and everybody's act should be judged favorably if they increased the victim's suffering which, however, also implies that no one should be so judged since ultimately nobody does anything to alleviate the sufferer's pain. In order to avoid this paradoxical result it might be necessary to grant the permission to cause human suffering only to a certain number of individuals but not to others, which would involve legislating different rules of behavior for different people. The alternative is to make a general rule among humans: never cause or condone suffering with the view that it provides opportunities for others to react virtuously.

The most crucial point, already very briefly alluded to at the end of Chapter 6 is this, however. It is not unreasonable to hold that A may be permitted to cause suffering to B with the view of

providing opportunities for virtuous response, only if A can
guarantee with absolute certainty that he will fully compensate B
for his present suffering. By 'fully compensate' I mean that B will
deem the experience of having been subjected to the suffering plus
the subsequent experience of receiving compensation preferable
to the experience of having neither. It is obvious that only God is
in the position to be able to do this.

CHAPTER 9

A NEW SOLUTION

The solution I now want to consider is based on a certain view of what constitutes good and evil, a view which is certainly not absurd or wholly arbitrary but in fact is a view to which many of us are prepared to subscribe. It is a solution which I had first vaguely and defectively advanced in the *American Philosophical Quarterly* (1964) pp. 244–47. With the passage of time, helped by the stimulus received from objections raised, the true nature of this somewhat complex solution gradually unfolded in my mind and I think I was able to provide a much improved account of it by the time I contributed to the discussion held in *The Journal of Value Inquiry* (1970). At this stage I feel that I may be able to present a clear enough exposition, so that the reader, who may initially be quite put off by the seeming strangeness of the solution, is by the end of the next chapter satisfied that yet another path has been opened toward the elimination of the problem of evil.

As a rule evil human acts are regarded as those acts which contravene moral obligations. This brings us at once to the question, what are my obligations toward my fellow man? On the surface it may seem that the most general kind of obligation I have toward another is to make him — provided this does not interfere with the welfare of others — as happy as I can. Upon reflection, however, this appears inadequate.

Suppose I had a child of very low intelligence but of very happy disposition under my care. When he grows up he is not going to know more than a few dozen words and perform a few easy manual tasks; but he will not mind, for provided his basic bodily needs are minimally taken care of, he enjoys lying on his back and staring into the air. A minor operation, I am assured by the best medical authorities, would spectacularly raise his intelligence and render him capable of creative achievements as well as appreciating music, art, literature, science and philosophy. Naturally, if his intelligence were raised, he would be vulnerable to the frustrations, disappointments and anxieties most of us are subject to from time to time. Should I leave him to grow up as a happy idiot or am I morally obliged to raise his intelligence? I believe it will be agreed that I should be reprehensible if I refrained from letting the child have the operation, even if I were in the position to insure that his physical needs would be always taken care of.

But why is it not good enough that I am keeping him in a state of maximum happiness? Apparently the degree of desirability of a state (DDS) is not a simple function of a single factor — namely the degree to which one's wants are satisfied — but is also dependent on the kind of being one is. The somewhat less happy, intelligent child is ultimately better off than the happy idiot because, although the factor of happiness is present, in his case less than in full amount, he is more than compensated for this by having become a more preferable kind of person.

This idea, that my moral obligations consist not simply in my having to endeavour to raise the amount of happiness a certain being is granted to enjoy, but that these obligations are somewhat more complex and consist of my having to raise his DDS, which is a two-valued function, depending both on the potentials of the individual and the amount to which his needs are being taken care of, is also illustrated by the following: In recent years much has been heard about machines one may get hooked up to and have the pleasure centers in one's brains electrically stimulated. Once a person's brain is connected to the machine he becomes completely captivated by the experience it provides and desires absolutely nothing but the passive enjoyment of the sublime pleasures induced by it. I believe that most people have the kind of value judgement according to which they would condemn me, if without prior consultation, I hooked up A — a normal person — to this machine and thus caused him to become addicted to it for the rest of his life. This would be so even if I provided an attendant to look after A's vital physical needs. I should, I believe, be severely condemned although A's addiction has no ill after-effects. But A, a previously normal person, has had his usual ups and downs, while now he is in a continual state of 'bliss'. Shouldn't I be praised for having eliminated the large gap between his potential and actual amount of happiness by having satiated him with pleasure?

The answer, I believe, is that I should not be praised, and not merely because I have rendered A a less useful member of society. Even if the needs of others are not taken into account it will be agreed by most that by inducing in A a permanent state of euphoria I have not done a good thing to him. This is so because I have reduced the desirability of A's state. The latter is not solely a function of how satiated A is with pleasure but also of the kind of being he is. A was, prior to my interference, capable of a great variety of response, of interaction with others, of creativity and self-improvement, while now he is reduced to a completely inactive, vegetable-like existence. The great increase in the factor of happiness is insufficient to make up for the great loss in the second factor — A being lowered from the state of a normal human being to the state of an inferior quasi-hibernating inert existence.

The general ethical view I am trying to explain, and which is quite widely accepted, is well reflected in the famous dictum by J.S. Mill, 'Better Socrates dissatisfied than the fool satisfied; better the fool dissatisfied than the pig satisfied.' It suggests that given two different creatures A and B, with different capacities and appetites and with different potentials for suffering and happiness, the desirability of their states are comparable on an absolute external criterion. It may turn out that A is satisfied with his lot while B is complaining, yet by this higher criterion, B is in a more desirable state than A. Accordingly, one of the universal rules of ethics is not, if everything else is equal increase the state of happiness of A, but rather, if everything is equal increase the degree of desirability of the state of A by as much as possible. It may be pointed out that generally I have far more oportunities to affect A's happiness than to affect the other factor which determines the degree of desirability of his state. It should also be noted that it is by no means always clear how much increase in one factor makes up for a given decrease in the other factor.

Now I take it that, conceptually, there is no limit to the degree which the desirability of state may reach. One can easily conceive a super-Socrates who has a much higher intelligence and many more than five senses through which to enjoy the world and who stands to Socrates like the latter stands to the pig. And there is the possibility of super-super-Socrates and so on *ad infinitum*. Given this last supposition about an infinite hierarchy of possible beings and hence the limitlessness of the possible increase in DDS, how does the aforementioned universal ethical rule apply to God '. . . increase the DDS as much as possible?' But no matter to what degree the desirability of state of a given being is increased it is always logically possible to increase it further. A mortal's possibilities are physically limited, hence there is, in his case, a natural limit which applies to the principle but there is no limit to what God can do. It is, therefore, logically impossible for him to fulfill the ethical principle, i.e., to do enough to discharge his obligation to raise the DDS of every creature to the height beyond which he cannot increase it. Just as it is logically impossible to name the highest integer, it is impossible to grant a creature a DDS higher than which is inconceivable; thus it is logically impossible for God to fulfill what is required by the universal ethical principle and therefore he cannot fulfill it, and is therefore not obliged to fulfill it. There is no room for complaint, seeing that God has not fulfilled the ethical principle which mortals are bound by and has left his creatures in various states of low desirability. Thus the problem of evil vanishes.

Before ending this Chapter I should like to remove at least one possible source of misunderstanding. While it does seem only too obvious that, because of the lack of limit to the ways in which a creature might be rendered capable of receiving all kinds of pleasures, the DDS that is reachable has, in principle, no end, the reader may still be troubled by the thought that nevertheless there just must be a state of highest DDS, namely that of God. Have not theologians declared the state enjoyed by God himself as the best conceivable and therefore constituting the upper limit of desirability? The answer is that the predicate 'perfect' has, of course, traditionally been applied to God. But when it is said that God is perfect what is meant, among other things, is that he is omnipotent, omniscient, omnibenevolent and immutable. It is by no means required to maintain that he also enjoys the highest DDS in the sense given to the term here. There is no need to think that God ever suffers or enjoys himself. But our notion of DDS is essentially a function of the capacity for suffering and enjoyment and the actual amount of suffering and enjoyment shared by a given creature. I maintain, therefore, that God does not enjoy the state of highest degree of desirability as defined in this chapter.

CHAPTER 10

THE REMOVAL OF OBJECTIONS
TO THE LAST SOLUTION

There is natural resistance to accepting this solution upon hearing it for the first time. It certainly provides no consolation for the sufferer to hear, not that his sad plight contains some ray of hope, that things are perhaps not as bad as they look, but that God has no obligations toward him. The solution also sounds highly paradoxical in that it claims that God, who can do so much more than human beings, is obliged to do less rather than more than a human being.

In order that the reader may find it gradually more acceptable, I shall attempt to shed more light on the present solution by answering a series of objections that have been raised against it by various people. Let me emphasize that my intention is not a polemical one and it is not at all my purpose to demonstrate how very misguided people have been in attacking my solution. I devote this chapter to the discussion of these objections in the firm conviction that it is a most efficient means of elucidating the proposed solution.

(1) Admittedly it is impossible that God should place everybody or, for that matter, anybody in a state better than which is inconceivable, for there is no limit to DDS. Yet he could improve the state of everybody and make it better than it is now. The problem of evil may thus be stated, not as the problem of why things are not so good that they could not be better, only why they are not better than they actually are. Among the people who have posed this question are Edward H. Madden and Peter H. Hare who ask:

The core of the problem of evil is not why God did not create a perfect world but why he did not create a better one.[1]

The obvious answer is that I am justified in complaining about an existing state of affairs only if what I am complaining about is not logically inherent in every state of affairs, that is, if the situation could be changed into another in which the reason for complaint would be removed. If, however, it is clear that no matter what changes are introduced, in any new situation there is exactly as much reason to complain as before, there is no right to demand that the present situation be replaced by another. In our case it is clear that no matter by how much the DDS of an individual be increased, it would still be just as short of being so high that higher it could not be, as it is now. Therefore, in any improved situation, objectively speaking, there is as much reason for complaint as there is in the present situation. So while the creatures' state could so be changed as to make them cease to complain, nothing could be done to mitigate the objective situation and remove the objective grounds in which to complain — namely that things are infinitely less good than they could be. The reason for this complaint remains constant through all changes; there is therefore no objective justification for demanding any changes.

The absurdity of the demand that God should have created a better world can be brought out also by asking what advice Madden and Hare would have given God had he consulted them prior to the creation of the world. They would not have advised 'create the best possible world' since they admit that there is no such possible world. Would they have urged him 'create a better world?' Better than what? Better than some world he could have created instead? That would be an empty advice since no matter what he does the resulting universe will be better than some he could have created. And surely they could not have advised him

[1]   *Evil and the Concept of God* (Springfield, Ill., 1968), p. 39.

'create a better universe than you are going to create'. It would then have to be agreed that, as far as the DDS of God's creatures is concerned, it matters not what world he creates.

(2)   A question formulated differently but which in essence is very similar to (1) has been posed by Nicholas La Para.[2] He points out that if we agree to apply, so far as possible, human ethical standards in our appraisal of Divine conduct, we should then consider a comparable situation in human affairs: what is required from a human agent who can perform but a fraction of a given morally desirable act? Two cases must be distinguished. Case one is where the performance of a part of the act achieves nothing; case two, where the partial act brings partial benefit. All will agree that in case one the agent is exempt from all action, for why should he be required to do anything that is of no value in itself? In case two, however, even though he cannot accomplish the whole task, nevertheless, since a part of it has some value too, he is not absolved from carrying it out. The situation facing God, says La Para, is of the second type. Even if he cannot create a universe better than which is not conceivable, he could have accomplished a fraction of that task and created a universe better than ours.

Now of course I agree that if the circumstances are comparable, human ethical standards are to be used in our appraisal of Divine conduct, and I also agree that a human agent who cannot perform a morally desirable act but can perform a small part of it, no matter how small, as long as it is of some use, is obliged to perform it. But what exactly are the obligations of such a person, what size part of the task does he have to accomplish? The answer, of course, is that a person who cannot accomplish a good deed in its entirely must do as great a part of it as he can. To apply this rule to God: since he cannot create the best of all possible worlds let him create as good a world as he can. But this makes as much

2   'Suffering, Happiness, and Evil', *Sophia* (1965).

sense as saying, since he cannot name the highest integer let him name an integer as high as he can. Or in brief: a human agent who can perform a part of a morally desirable act as he was required to do is free from further obligations, but God, were he to create a better world than ours, would still not satisfy La Para who would have just as much reason as before to demand that he create a yet better world.

(3) But let God as least eliminate all suffering, asks La Para.[3] Jay F. Rosenberg asks a question in similar vein. He expounds his objection in greater detail in his paper 'The Problem of Evil Revisited: A Reply to Schlesinger'.[4] He claims that one of the supreme rules of ethics is that one must not allow a gap between a creature's actual and potential amount of happiness. According to this, God is allowed to choose to create all sorts of creatures with different appetites and capacities for happiness but then he has to see to it that everybody's potential for happiness is fully saturated. This is possible to achieve but in our world it is not achieved. Hence, God is blameworthy.

It is quite possible that Rosenberg's rule will appeal to some people. However, as I have explained before, the present solution is based on a different rule of ethics which requires something else, namely, never decrease, always endeavour to increase everybody's DDS by as much as possible. Once we accept this rule rather than Rosenberg's, it can no longer be maintained that, if God had created a world in which nobody suffers or in which everybody's potential for happiness is fully saturated, then there would be no room for complaint. It has, after all, been explained that when A and B are in different states and A is complaining while B is entirely satisifed with his lot, it is not necessarily the case that B is better off than A. 'Better a fool dissatisfied than a pig satisfied, etc'. It would, therefore, be absurd to say that if a being were left

---

[3] *Ibid.*
[4] *The Journal of Value Inquiry* (1970).

to exist as a low order creature but satisfied, then his case would represent no evil, while if he were placed in what is objectively a more preferable state, namely, were turned into a much higher order creature, though not entirely satisfied, then one can justifiably complain about the evil in the world.

(4) At one stage Rosenberg explicitly criticizes the ethical principle which underlies the solution under discussion

'. . .Schlesinger assumes not only that there is a smooth continuum of states of increasing individual preferability but also that this continuum corresponds exactly to one of increasing *moral* desirability. As he explicitly put it elsewhere:

> Once we agree that the value of all moments of experience of each individual can fully be represented by points on a linear scale (of any two moments the one preferable to the other being represented by a point lying to the right of the point representing the others) *it follows* that to be morally good is to cause everyone's pointer to lie as much to the right on his line as possible.

("Omnipotence and Evil: An Incoherent Problem", *Sophia*, 1965, pp. 21–24) But the moral point of view is not thus directly constructible from individual desirability characterizations. To cite just one example: There is no doubt that an incarcerated criminal would find the freedom consequent upon unobstructed escape *preferable* to his life in prison. Yet to permit the escape which moves his pointer to the right is to commit a moral wrong.'[5]

To answer this objection we have to remind ourselves of the idea – with which Rosenberg himself seems to be in full agreement in the rest of his paper – that the desirability of a state does not depend on how much the subject desires to be in that state. The satisfied fool is satisfied to remain in his state and does not desire at all to be transformed into a dissatisfied Socrates, even though from an objective point of view that would be an improvement. The fact that the criminal prefers to be free rather than imprisoned does not mean that freedom is preferable to him in the relevant sense. Assuming that spending time in a prison does have

---

[5] *Ibid.*, p. 218n.

a reforming effect, then from an objective point of view it is worthwhile to suffer loss of freedom and be compensated for it by becoming a reformed, better person.

In addition, it must be also emphasized that the unqualified rule, always avoid decreasing, and endeavour to increase the degree of a given creature's state of desirability, applies only if this does not interfere with the state of other creatures. Thus, even if it were better for the criminal to remain at large rather than be incarcerated, if he would be set free this would greatly decrease the DDS of others whom he might harm. Also, his going un-punished will encourage others to commit crimes, resulting in a great loss of DDS for a large number of people.

(5) It is a fact that when we witness Socrates positively dis-tressed, or even just deprived from the happiness he could partake in, our compassion is aroused. On the other hand we are not in the least upset when we see a satisfied pig. Does this not show that we tend not to subscribe to the view expounded here concerning the degree of desirability of a state being a two valued function? Does this not show that what really seems to matter to us is whether a creature's actual needs, whatever they may be, are satisfied, but not what kind of a creature a given individual is?

First of all let me say that it really does not matter so much what we actually find emotionally upsetting and what not, as long as the ethical point of view on which our solution is based can be fully described, and when described, is not found incoherent, arbitrary or absurd. But the story concerning the retarded child and the story about the pleasure machine show more than that, they show, as I have argued in the previous chapter, that the ethical point of view in question is not merely explainable, but is even the one to which we all find ourselves subscribing in different contexts. The apparent counter-example just cited seems to arise only because in practice there is very little mobility across the boundaries between various kinds of creatures. An inferior crea-ture is taken for granted to be what he is and not someone who could be and therefore perhaps ought to be a higher kind of creature. Let us imagine, however, that we have witnessed Socrates deprived of all his belongings, prohibited from studying or engaging in discussion and thrown out of his house. Subsequently there comes along a magician who turns Socrates into a pig, thus rendering him satisfied to do nothing all day long but roll in the mud and eat. It seems to me that we would not regard his problems as having been solved but, on the contrary, feel intense pity that an accomplished being like Socrates has been reduced to such a state that he does not feel at all the great deprivations he has been subjected to, as deprivations.

(6) A question in similar vein is posed by Madden and Hare. They say:

It is understandable if a mother is grief-stricken because her child is killed, but it is not understandable if she is grief-stricken because her child is not as bright as Einstein.[6]

Being grief-stricken is very much a function of what is usual and therefore unexpected. Since it is normal for a child to be less bright than Einstein, people find it acceptable. But if all children born were at least as bright as Einstein, then the only mother whose child turns out to have what in our world amounts to an I.Q. of 100, would regard it an exceptional disaster and would be very grief-stricken. Also, if it was an immutable law of nature that everybody's third child was killed at the age of ten, then a mother of a ten-year-old third child who was killed, would find this much more acceptable than she would in our world. But this has not much to do with what is good and what is evil from an absolute point of view. If God created a world in which everybody without exception was kept constantly in the same low desirability of state — fools, living in a fool's paradise — nobody would complain, but this would not render that world into the best of

---

[6] *Evil and the Concept of God*, p. 39.

all possible worlds.

(7)   A very pertinent question is asked by La Para, who claims that if we agree that every universe God could create would necessarily be imperfect, it does not follow that it is of no moral consequence whatever he does. On the contrary, the impossibility of a perfect world imposes upon him to do specifically one thing and one thing alone: not to create anything. Once again he employs human analogy to show that if in creating any world in which there are living beings God renders himself blameworthy, then refraining from all creation, he should be free from all blame. He says:

'. . .imagine that astrologers really can foretell what the consequences of our actions will be. Suppose, further, that their family astrologer tells a man and wife that if they so choose, they will conceive a child on March first. But this, child, while he would have no effect on the happiness or suffering of his contemporaries, would himself lead a wretched life, one filled with physical and psychological torment. Alternatively, if the couple so choose, they will conceive a child on March second. Now this child, who also would not effect the happiness of those around him would himself enjoy a life of sublime contentment and pleasure. If this couple decide to conceive a child on March first they are obviously open to moral reproach. If however, they decide to conceive a child on March second they certainly would not be open to reproach. But if they decide to refrain altogether from having children have they incurred any blame? Not at all. It would be ridiculous to say this to the couple. "You are evil, for by refraining from conceiving a child on March second you failed to bring about as much happiness in him as you might have." Similarly, if an omnipotent being once created a world, he could then be reproached for failing to make it as good a world as he might have. But it is ridiculous to imagine that an omnipotent being might be morally reprehensible because he refrained from creating at all.'[7]

One can answer La Para by saying that God could not have refrained from creating altogether since there are certain Divine goals which must be attained. These goals include the existence of beings capable of contemplating moral values, asserting their free will and exercising compassion, charity, fortitude, humility,

---

[7]   'Suffering, Happiness and Evil', *Sophia* (1965), pp. 15—16.

forgiveness, justice and so on.

While this answer is entirely sufficient, for a better understanding of the issues at hand it is important to point out that we do not need it. La Para after all, seems to be involved in a contradiction. He will surely agree that the absolute absence of any creation cannot be regarded as the best of all possible worlds, and just as there are infinitely many kinds of universes that represent worse states of affairs than complete void so there are infinitely many which are better. But how then can La Para escape the accusation that he holds, that in infinitely many instances what is more desirable is less desirable. After all, there are infinitely many peopled universes which represent more desirable states of affairs than that in which nothing exists. Yet he claims if God brings forth any of these universes, he is blameworthy, while when permitting a less desirable situation to prevail — the existence of nothing — he is free of blame.

It may seem for a moment that I now contradict my previous claim that the problem of evil is independent of the amount of suffering we find in the world. It is after all the amount of suffering in a possible world that determines whether it is better than a void or worse than a void. Hence, if it were the case that there is on balance so much evil in the actual world that a void would be better, the argument from evil works.

But of course, as soon as we agree that complete void is also a state of affairs which has to be assigned a certain point j on the DDS-line then we can no longer maintain that it is a Divine duty to bring about this situation. For why should we be satisfied if God stops at j; why should he not be asked to create a state of affairs whose DDS is at k far to the right of j, and so on. It follows therefore, that whatever, the DDS of the actual world is, whether represented by i, a point far off to the left of j or by k, there is never any room for complaint.

On the surface it may seem that La Para has an answer to this, for he might try to explain away the seeming contradiction of his position by claiming that moral obligations do not exist in a vacuum but only in relation to a subject. For every X, if X is a living creature, my obligation toward him is to cause his 'welfare pointer' to be shifted as much to the right as I can. In case of a non-existent X, however, there is no-one toward whom I may be said to have moral obligations. Thus, even if it is a certainty that for some X, by bringing X into being I can guarantee a life in which every moment is preferable to a state of non-existence, no one binds me to bring X into being.

But La Para cannot hold this and at the same time maintain that the couple who decide to conceive a child on March first is open to moral reproach. After all, they have no obligation to the yet unborn child not to bring him into this world. He would thus have to modify his stand saying that although I have no obligations toward non-existent beings, if my acts have results about which some existent being eventually may have just cause to complain, I must refrain from performing them. The couple, conceiving a child on March first, place themselves in a situation where they will be blamed by a child for having brought him into the world; they must therefore refrain from the act of conception. But, if so, it stands to reason that, if an act has results for which someone later will have just cause for praising me then I am doing a morally desirable act in performing it and incur blame for not performing it. Thus, since if the couple conceives a child on March second, the resulting individual will have cause for praising them for having brought him into the world, if they refrain from conceiving a child on March second, they should be open to reproach.

It seems, therefore, that La Para's description of the moral situation of the couple, who are advised by their astrologer, was not correct. We were inclined to agree with him that the couple is not obliged to bring a child into the world because indeed, under normal circumstances this is so. But under normal circumstances one could never know for sure that a child about to be born is going to lead a completely happy life in which every moment his

DDS would be above the point associated with non-existence. And even if it were possible to foretell with certainty that a child about to be conceived is going to be happy all his life, no obligation to bring him into this world would exist, since the rule to increase a given individual's DDS as much as you can only applies without reservation when by doing so, you do not adversely affect the state of others. Bringing a completely happy individual into this world carries no guarantee that it will positively affect the DDS of other people. In the extraordinary situation described by La Para in which we are in a position to know that the child would enjoy a very happy life and also that he would not affect the happiness of others, we simply cannot rely on our intuitions which are derived from fundamentally different situations. The correct answer therefore may be that the couple would be morally obliged to conceive a child on March second.

(8) Probably the best of all the objections that have come to my attention has been raised by Winslow Shea.[8] He points out that according to the suggested solution it makes absolutely no difference in which state the inhabitants of this world are, the problem of evil simply does not arise, since no matter what, nothing can be done which would bring anybody's state nearer to the state which could not be improved any further. But being good essentially implies that one does certain things and refrains from others; yet God's goodness turns out not to impose upon him any restraints at all. He is completely free to do anything to anyone, for no matter what he does we cannot attribute evil to him. This may provide grounds for exonerating God from evil no matter what we observe, but surely we cannot go further — as is required by the theist — and positively attribute goodness to him. For in what sense can one attribute goodness to God? Does the belief that he is good have any substance when such a belief does

---

[8] 'God, Evil and Professor Schlesinger', *Journal of Value Inquiry*, (1970), pp. 219−28.

not render one at all capable of foretelling what sorts of things God will do and what he will refrain from doing? Is the predicate 'good' not empty of all meaning as applied to God when this application carries no implications as to what acts are and what are not compatible with his nature?

Or, to put it differently, if the world was governed by an absolutely evil monster, it does not seem that our observations would have to be different from what they are now. An omni-malevolent being might leave the world in the state it is without turning anyone into a lower kind of creature or increase the amount of his suffering, by the same kind of argument we have used before: no matter how bad things are they can always be worse; it is logically impossible to be in a state worse than which is inconceivable; any situation is therefore bad enough to be permitted by an omnimalevolent being. But if the same state of affairs is compatible with the world being governed by an omni-benevolent and an omnimalevolent being, what feature of the world permits us to meaningfully assert that it was created by the former rather than by the latter? Do we not have to conclude that the notions of omnibenevolence and omnimalevolence are inter-changeable as well as devoid of all meaning?

This last objection, if valid, implies that my attempted defense of Divine goodness made things worse than they were before: the atheist claimed only that God is, in fact, not perfectly good since evil has been observed to exist, but on my analysis one has to conclude that he cannot necessarily be good at all since the notion of goodness logically cannot apply to an omnipotent being.

However the objection would have been valid only if it were a fact that the sole rule goodness imposes upon its practitioners is to increase the DDS of everyone by as much as possible. Now while this rule is very central there are many other rules as well and omnipotence is compatible with these. A good being, for example, may be expected to be truthful most of the time, and a perfectly good being, irrespective of how powerful, can be relied upon to be truthful every time. Religions based on revelation claim that God made certain promises. Because of his omnibenevolence it is absolutely certain that all his promises will be fulfilled.

Nor does there seem to be any excuse why, if the world is governed by an Almighty God, there should be even a single case of injustice in it. Omnipotence certainly does not interfere with the ability to be perfectly just; on the contrary it guarantees it. One who believes in a perfect God is committed to the belief that perfect justice reigns in the world, which implies that whenever the degree of the desirability of someone is raised or lowered as a reward or punishment for his behavior, the amount of raising or lowering is uniformly proportional to the weight of his acts. That this is not so of course, has, not been demonstrated. It has already been seen before that once it is postulated that an individual's existence does not terminate with his physical death, provision has been made for any imbalance in recompense to correct itself. But now a further factor ensuring the impossibility of detecting any injustice in this world, has been introduced. The present solution permits the imparting of suffering and pleasure without regard to an individual's merits. Only in some instances is it true — and we may not know in which — that a person is subjected to pain or joy for the purpose of castigating or rewarding him.

It is also possible to see the manifestation of Divine goodness in the fact that all God's creatures who are capable of value judgements have been endowed with free will to embrace or reject those values. The possession of free will by sentient beings is highly desirable on its own as said before, and it is desirable, in a sense different from that given to the term 'desirability', that features in the notion of DDS. The latter, as I have already pointed out, is a function of the capacity of partaking in various kinds of pleasures and pains and the actual amount of these imparted to a given individual.

(9) Another point of Shea in the same paper, is that in order to embrace my solution one has to renounce Leibniz's claim that

ours is the best of all possible worlds.

Now to the question of whether Leibniz's theodicy is available to us the answer is both yes and no; but where Leibniz's solution is not available it is not needed and where needed it is available. It is obvious that the problem of evil exists if the notion of the best of all possible worlds is coherent and our world happens not to instantiate it. In some respects 'the best of all possible worlds' is incoherent and in others it is not, for some things do not admit maximization while others do. There can be no world in which all creatures are, or indeed any creature is, in a state of maximum desirability. It makes no sense, therefore, to complain that the degree of desirability of X's state is much less than the maximum. Thus with respect to the DDS creatures possess this is not the best of all possible worlds because it cannot be the best of all possible worlds and need not be the best of all possible worlds. On the other hand, a world in which perfect justice prevails is not logically impossible. A single clearly demonstrated case of injustice would, therefore, present a real difficulty for theism as was already recognized in early antiquity. With respect to justice a best of all possible worlds is possible and the theist believes the existing world is such.

(10) Finally, I should mention that Haig Khatchadourian has also written an article devoted to criticising our solution.[9] I shall not say too much about it since a number of points he has raised have already been answered and others, I must confess, I do not quite understand. For example, he objects to my contention that there seem to be infinite possibilities for happiness. Among others he points out that increasing the possibilities for happiness entails increasing the possibilities for unhappiness. I just cannot imagine why he thought this constituted an objection. He also says:

'. . .our biological and psychological make-up as human beings appears to place limitations on our capacity for experiencing happiness. At any rate,

[9] 'God, Happiness and Evil', *Religious Studies* (1966), pp. 109–19.

even if this is not the case, our nature together with the nature of the universe (e.g. the laws of nature) appears to place limitations on the *number* and *kinds* of possibilities for happiness which are open to us, and perhaps to other beings of similar nature.'[10]

This objection, however, loses its point once we realize that what is relevant to my argument is not physical but logical possibilities. There is undoubtedly a very good *prima facie* case for saying that, given a creature capable of a certain range of pleasurable experience, it is always possible to conceive of another who is capable of a larger range. For example, a creature with n separate pairs of ears leading to n separate compartments of his brain that receive musical impressions, seems conceivable. Hence, a creature capable of listening simultaneously to n different orchestras playing n different concerts and enjoying them separately seems logically possible. The same creature's DDS would definitely increase if n was increased to $n + 1$ and at the same time he was allowed to enjoy listening to $n + 1$ orchestras playing $n + 1$ concerts. The onus of proof would be on anyone claiming that what was just said was logically incoherent.

To conclude with a most important point: Khatchadourian complains that my claim that an omnipotent being who can do so much more than ordinary mortals has less, and not more, moral obligations than such finite beings is 'downright paradoxical'. As I already had an opportunity to remark at the beginning of this chapter, I fully agree that at first one is indeed bound to receive an impression of paradoxicality and this very fact may be responsible for putting many critics into an unreceptive frame of mind to our solution.

But we should remind ourselves that it is the nature of things, and it has been accepted for long as such, that in certain respects an omnipotent being is capable of doing less than a finite creature. An often cited example is the fact that you and I may be able to

---

[10] *Ibid.*, p. 14.

put together a thing so heavy that we cannot lift it but an omnipotent being is not capable of creating a stone so heavy that he himself cannot lift it. At any rate, after thoroughly inspecting the arguments laid out in the last two chapters and finding that they are based on assumptions which are not themselves strange, the initial impression that our conclusion is paradoxical should disappear.

We began our inquiries by explaining that the problem of evil may be represented by the schema

$$[\{(H \& A \& A') \to O \} \& \sim O \& A \& A'] \to - H$$

where   H = An omnipotent and omnibenevolent being exists.
  A = Benevolence precludes the perpetuating or condoning of suffering.
  A' = There are no morally sufficient reasons for God to permit suffering.
  O = Suffering does not exist.

Now it is undeniable that (H&A&A') → O; it has, in fact, been observed that ~ O; A simply expresses the meaning of 'benevolence' unless the suffering in question is necessary. It has been pointed out that A' cannot certainly be known to be true but there are very strong *prima facie* reasons to think this to be so. Hence ~ H had to be regarded as strongly confirmed. This has provided the firmest ground upon which theism has been attacked.

From what has been said in the last seven chapters it becomes evident that the atheist is not standing on firm ground when using the fact of the existence of suffering as a tool to demolish theism. We have seen that there are at least three different ways in which it can be reasonably maintained that A' is in fact false. It would be dogmatic to insist that theism had been disconfirmed by claiming it to be irrational to subscribe to any of the presuppositions required by the three solutions.

PART II

FREE WILL, MEN AND MACHINES

CHAPTER 11

A CONFLICT BETWEEN RELIGION AND SCIENCE

So far we have had several opportunities to mention the claim that religion requires that some human choices are, in principle, unpredictable. First, it was in connection with the notion of reward and punishment which are not justified unless people could be held responsible for their actions. This implies that people have free will and many philosophers take this to mean that some human choices are, in principle, unpredictable. Then, in two different contexts, the question was raised why God does not create only such men whom he knows in advance will never choose to do evil and the answer, to which a very great number of philosophers subscribe, is that the freedom of men entails that even God cannot exactly predict what they might do. In addition, in the last chapter we claimed that God's benevolence expresses itself in creating agents endowed with free will. In short, a great majority of theists insist, for a variety of reasons, that human dignity and autonomy, and man's status of having been created in the image of God — through the benevolence of the latter — and the fact people are held responsible for the way they conduct their lives demand that at least some human choices are basically unpredictable.

Modern science, however, paints a different picture of man. It is not that there is some specific scientific result which is in conflict with the postulate of free will, but rather that the doctrine of determinism, interpreted as claiming that given all the initial conditions and all the laws of nature, every event is predictable, conflicts with this postulate. Again, determinism is not a confirmed scientific hypothesis but many scientists regard it as part of an enlightened scientific attitude to assume that the universe is fully governed by deterministic laws. It is, after all, a fact that with the

advance of science many phenomena have increasingly been discovered to be governed by deterministic laws and extrapolating
from the past successes of science, scientists, in general, have come
to believe that all events are governed by deterministic laws and
are predictable in principle. As early as 1820, with the complete
success of celestial mechanics to account for all the movements of
the planets, Laplace declared that for an intelligence acquainted
with the position of all material particles and with the forces
acting between them, all the events of the future would be present
to his eyes.[1] Admittedly this view has suffered a setback with the
advent of quantum mechanics and the discovery of the uncertain-
ty principle according to which there are occurrences not determined by any laws and which are, in principle, unpredictable. In
general however, it is still believed that macroscopic phenomena
are entirely subject to deterministic laws and this includes all brain
events which are relevant to human behavior such as the firing of
neurons. At any rate, it has been the central aim of modern
psychology to discover all the laws governing human behavior,
showing it to be entirely predictable. We have here, then, a basic
conflict between religion and science.

[1] *Théorie analytique des probabilités*, Paris (1820), Preface.

CHAPTER 12

NEWCOMB'S PROBLEM OF CHOICE

I

In order to resolve the problem just stated and make a number of other important points concerning the question of the confirmation of the theistic hypothesis I have to discuss a topic whose relevance, I promise, will quite soon become apparent.

I shall begin with a story concerning a being who has shown himself capable on a million occasions in the past, of predicting human choices with perfect accuracy and is therefore generally considered as a perfect predictor of such choices. Let us assume that the use to which he wants to put his extraordinary powers is to try and restrain human greediness. The particular way in which he attempts to reform the world is by placing two boxes in front of people half an hour before t_1 and allowing them the choice — after half an hour's deliberation — to:

C_1 : choose to take box II only

or

C_2 : choose to take both boxes

and punish those who for whatever reason do choose C_2. He achieves his aim at t_0, 24 hours prior to t_1, by sealing both boxes after having put $1000 in box I and after having put $1 000 000 ($M) in box II if and only if:

P_1 : he predicts that at t_1 the agent does C_1

or after having put nothing in box II if and only if:

P_2 : he predicts that at t_1 the agent does C_2.

Consider how the situation of an agent who knows everything I have said so far and wants to maximize his gain. There is an argument based on the belief in the phenomenal powers of the predictor that the agent should restrain himself and do C_1 so as to end up with \$M like all the 500 000 people in the past who have picked box II only, rather than do C_2 and end up with a mere \$1000. But there is also an argument leading to the conclusion that it is best to do C_2. Some people thought[1] that what is called the 'dominance argument' leads to this conclusion and hence we are faced with the problem that we have an argument that it is best to do C_1, as well as an argument that it is best to do C_2 and this problem has become known as 'Newcomb's problem of choice'. The truth, however, is that the dominance argument does not lead to such a conclusion. It is important to see why. The dominance argument runs as follows: there are two possibilities, P_1 and P_2. Now should it be a fact that P_1, then by doing C_2 the agent surely wins in addition to \$M the \$1000 of box I and thus is better off than if he did C_1. But if P_2 is the case, then he is also better off by doing C_2. So in either case he is better off doing C_2 than C_1, thus C_2 is his best choice.

But what is obviously wrong with this argument is that its premisses, namely that by doing C_2 the agent is better off than when, given the same state of the boxes, he does C_1, are quite compatible with the hypothesis that the predictor is perfect. And the trouble is that there is an argument from this hypothesis to the conclusion that the agent should do C_1, which appears to contradict the conclusion of the dominance argument. For given this hypothesis, there are only two situations possible: (a) P_1 & C_1, in which case the agent is *worse off* as compared to the situation in which it remained P_1 but he did C_2 (for then he would gain \$1 001 000 instead of merely \$M, as he does now); (b) P_2 & C_2,

---

[1]   cf. Robert Nozick 'Newcomb's Problem and Two Principles of Choice', *Essays in Honor of Carl G. Hempel*, ed. N. Rescher (Dordrecht, 1970), p.118.

in which case he is better off compared to the situation in which it remained P_2 but he did C_1 (for now he gets at least \$1000). Now because of the dominance argument, he is assured that by doing C_2 he places himself in a situation properly designated as 'better off'. But the only such situation available is (b). Thus, by doing C_2, he makes sure that the situation is (b) rather than (a). But it so happens that of the two available situations, (a) is preferable to (b) for to be 'worse off' relative to P_1 is preferable to being 'better off' relative to P_2, and he should therefore do C_1 rather than C_2.

To put it slightly differently: the argument based on the assumption that the predictor is perfect, and the dominance argument, are not really in conflict. The former leads to the conclusion that by doing C_1 the agent is assured that the best among all the *available* situations is realized. The dominance argument does not deny this. It claims only that when P_1 holds then C_2 ensures a better outcome for the agent than does C_1, and similarly for when P_2 holds. But that is quite compatible with C_1 being the best choice of all if the ability to make certain choices under certain conditions is removed.

Another way of proving quite conclusively that the dominance argument for doing C_2 must be wrong is to consider briefly another situation which obtains, which I shall call Game 2 (while the previous game I shall refer to as Game 1). In Game 2 the player has the same two choices as in Game 1, and while once more box I contains \$1000, box II is definitely empty. Instead of a predictor there is an observer who, if he observes that the agent has taken box II only, gives the player \$M and if he observes that he has taken both boxes he gives him nothing. The great difference between Game 1 and 2 is that the latter, unlike the former, does not require anything unavailable in practice. Unlike perfect predictors, there is no shortage of people competent to observe whether an agent has taken one or two boxes, thus any two people (with lowered stakes if necessary) can play Game 2. Should anybody have any doubts as to what the player's best choice is, let him play Game 2 several times and he will find out. At any rate I do not believe anyone would hesitate in the least to agree that obviously to maximize his gain the player should take the second box only.

Surprisingly enough however the dominance argument for doing C_2, that is for concluding that the greater advantage lies in taking both boxes, seems to apply here no less than in Game 1. Even now before making his choice, the agent knows that either of two propositions is true, (1) the observer will give him $M or (2) the observer will give him nothing. Now should it be a fact that (1) is true then by doing C_2, the agent surely wins in addition to $M the $1000 of box I and thus is better off than if he did C_1. But if (2) is true then also he is better off by doing C_2. So in either case he is better off doing C_2 than C_1, thus C_2 is his best choice. For whatever reason the reader believes that the argument must be fallacious, for the same reason the argument is fallacious also when applied to Game 1.

II

There is however a different, valid argument for taking both boxes in Game 1, an argument which cannot be applied to Game 2, Suppose a person who is sufficiently intelligent and to whom we shall refer as the 'perfect judge', is allowed to look at the contents of box II. This person is not allowed to communicate with the player though in his heart he may contemplate the best choice for the agent. If he sees that the box is empty he will surely deem C_2 as best, so that the agent gets at least a thousand dollars. If he sees that there is money in box II he will still deem the taking of both boxes as the best choice since he knows that by doing so the agent will not make money disappear from the box, something that has never happened before and would violate the laws of nature. (The exception is the case where the judge believes in the infallibility of the predictor, when he will sadly conclude that his sound judgement is surely going to be disregarded.) It follows, therefore, that even though the judge is not allowed to communicate with the player, the player knows with absolute certainty what his opinion is: it is best to take both boxes. It logically follows, that it is best for him to take both boxes. It is self-contradictory to assert that it may not be in my best interest to follow what in the opinion of a sufficiently well-informed and intelligent judge,[2] whose opinion by definition represents the truth, is not in my interest to follow; it would amount to saying that that which is in my best interest is not in my best interest. Now it does not matter that in fact there is no such judge at hand, since it is certain that if there was such a judge he would advise the player, no matter what, to take both boxes. It is necessarily true that it is in the best interest of the player to adopt what would be the best choice in the opinion of a sufficiently well-informed and intelligent judge, if he existed.

We have here then a solid deductive argument that in order to maximize his gain, the agent should take both boxes in accordance with the opinion of the perfect judge. It would be quite useless to try to argue, as some people have tried, that probabilities are relative to one's state of knowledge and that the player's state of knowledge is different to that of the perfect judge. Hence, while relative to the judge's information that it is certainly best to take both boxes, this may not be so relative to the inferior state of knowledge of the player. Relative to the player's knowledge — which is all that is, after all, available to him so the argument

---

[2] By 'sufficiently well informed' I mean no more than that he knows what is in Box II at the time he examines its contents as well as that there is $1000 in box I. By 'intelligent' I mean only that he has the trivial ability to realize that $x + 1,000 > x$. It would be exceedingly implausible to deny the possibility of the existence of a judge who qualifies as perfect by being merely so modestly endowed. This would become even more difficult in view of the point I shall make later that there is no reason why the predictor himself should not serve as the judge!

would go — the probability is virtually one that he is better off by taking box II only. This argument is wrong since, although it is true that the player lacks the information concerning the basis upon which the perfect judge advises him to take both boxes, this information is entirely irrelevant for him. It is sufficient for him to know for sure that his friend, who is completely reliable, believes it is better for him to take both boxes. Relative to this information alone it is already an absolute certainty that indeed it is better for him to take both boxes.[3]

We have arrived then at a contradiction: the infallibility of the predictor implies that in order to maximize his gain the player should choose to take box II only, but the argument from the perfect judge leads to the contrary conclusion, that he should take both boxes.

---

[3] In the *Australasian Journal of Philosophy* (1976) I have employed a different argument called the 'invincible player's strategy argument' to prove that C_2 must be the best choice. I shall, however, spare the reader the need to go through yet another argument in favor of C_2, when the one presented here will be seen fully effective on its own.

CHAPTER 13

THE UNPREDICTABILITY OF
SOME HUMAN CHOICES

I

It is a well known rule of logic that when one tells a story and that story eventually leads to a contradiction then it follows by *reductio* that the story was an impossible one to begin with. But what element in our story must be rejected as impossible? Is it impossible to place two boxes before a player etc.? Surely not. The most likely candidate for rejection is the assertion which did not amount to the description of an observed fact but which we *thought* was based on inductive evidence, namely that the predictor is virtually infallible as evidenced by his past performance. (It will turn out in Chapter 15 that it is not the case that the proficiency of the predictor *qua* predictor could ever be established by any evidence.) We shall deny, then, that our so called predictor has great powers of prediction.

It may perhaps seem that one could resist our conclusion. Admittedly the statement 'Under certain circumstances it may happen that it is not in my best interest to do what, in the opinion of a sufficiently intelligent and well informed observer, is best for me to do' is necessarily false. Nevertheless it does not follow that it is in the best interest of the player to do what would be advised by a person who is allowed to peep and see the contents of the second box. Contrary to his opinion, it may be more advantageous for the player to take box II only. The reason being that the so-called perfect judge is not well informed. Suppose he sees a million dollars in box II. His opinion is then, that the player ought to take both boxes so that he acquires more than a million dollars. If however, the player were to follow his advice the million dollars would vanish from box II and contrary to what he thought, the player would end up with a thousand dollars only. That this is what would happen is guaranteed by the fact that the predictor is indeed infallible and hence capable of ensuring that the second box is empty if the player takes both boxes. True enough in the past this has never happened: whenever the predictor put money into the second box it invariably remained there until it was opened by the player. It is also given that the boxes are completely sealed and well guarded and it is a well established fact that money does not disappear just like that from such boxes. All this, however, amounts to no more than a strong inductive argument why the well-wisher is well informed and why, if he sees a million dollars in box II, then there is very firm rational basis for believing that by taking both boxes one ends up with $1 000 000. However, we have already agreed that in order to avoid a contradiction we are compelled to reject a conclusion based on inductive reasoning. (At the moment we still assume that there *is* inductive evidence that the prediction is infallible.) Why is it obvious that we must reject the contention that the predictor is endowed with special powers, why not reject the assumption that a million dollars placed in box II do not spontaneously disappear?

The answer that might first spring to mind is that indeed all we know for sure from the fact that we have to avoid a contradiction, is that some inductively arrived-at conclusion must be given up but it is not directly indicated which one of such conclusions must be given up. In such a situation it is obvious that we should reject the conclusion which is not as strongly supported as any other. The conclusion that the predictor possesses a special ability is based on the evidence of his past performance, which has been postulated to be very extensive. On the other hand, the conclusion that once a million dollars are put in a well sealed box they do not just vanish, is based not only on our past experience with all the instances of Game 1 but on a vastly wide range of cases in the past in all of which items enclosed in well protected containers did not spontaneously disappear. If we were to decide to entertain the possibility of the disappearance of money from firmly sealed boxes we would have to modify many other well established theories concerning the properties of matter. Maintaining, however, that the predictor is powerless to foresee the choice the player is about to make does not require surrendering any other confirmed theory.

But there is also a much more important answer. As the reader might have guessed by now, the purpose of our story was to show that some human choices are unpredictable and this we would have succeeded in showing anyhow. For suppose that indeed if there is \$M in box II and the player then proceeds to do C_2, then the money will disappear from the second box. Should this really happen then we would still be forced to conclude that the predictor cannot predict free choices, since the only way he ensures that the player who takes both boxes does not get the million dollars, is not by anticipating his choice and therefore not putting any money in the second box right from the beginning, but by making the money disappear from the box upon seeing what the players choice is. Admittedly our predictor would still have to be endowed with a special gift to accomplish this feat, but it is not the gift of foreseeing the future.

It may also seem for a moment that one could object by saying that although the opinion of the 'perfect judge' to do C_2 must be correct, it cannot always be put into practice, since given that the predictor is infallible, when there is money in box II, the player just cannot take both boxes.

But the player must ask himself: is it in his best interest to take both boxes? The answer to this question must be, yes, since the perfect judge says so, or would say so. Hence he must try and take both boxes. Should he indeed find that he is just incapable of doing so, then there is immediate proof that we are not confronted here with an infallible predictor of free choices, since the way in which he ensures that his prediction, that the agent will take box II, comes true is by forcing him, if necessary against his will, to do so. On the other hand, if he feels that he is capable of taking both boxes, he should certainly do so for it is in his best interest, given that this is what the perfect well-wisher advises. But if, taking both boxes is indeed what leads to the maximization of gain, then the predictor cannot be infallible. The significant conclusion we wanted to reach was that there is some situation in which a free choice − i.e., a choice not made against one's will − is, in principle, impossible to predict and this seems to follow either way.

At this stage the reader may remind us of the two ways in which we refuted the dominance argument for doing C_2 in the last chapter and he may try applying them here too. First he might argue:[1] Admittedly the advice of the observer who is completely competent to judge the matter cannot be wrong. But it must be remembered that his advice to take both boxes may be prompted by his having observed two entirely different situations. It may be that he sees that there is money in box II and hence his advice is that you might as well gain an extra thousand dollars, but it is also possible that the observer sees that there is no money in box II and he advises taking both boxes so that the agent does not end up entirely empty handed. By taking both boxes the agent may bring about the second situation and for this reason he has to refrain from taking both boxes.

But of course, if we maintain this, our conclusion is that by taking both boxes the agent worsens his situation and that by taking box II only, he improves it. We can, however, pose this very question to the sufficiently well-informed competent judge: is there any point in exercising restraint and not taking box I? Does the agent in the least increase his chance of finding $M in box II by taking that box only? And we can work out with absolute

---

[1] James Cargile did actually argue this way in his 'Newcomb's Problem' in the *British Journal for the Philosophy of Science* (1975).

certainty the answer of the observer: there is absolutely nothing to gain by taking box II only. It is in the best interest for the agent to base his actions on the judgement of the observer.

His second objection would be this: what about Game 2 in which box I is left empty and our agent's playmate is not a predictor but one who gives him $M or nothing *after* the agent has done C_1 or C_2? Have we not agreed that it is indisputably clear in this case that C_1 is the best choice?

The answer is that indeed in Game 2 it is best to do C_1, but while with respect to the applicability of the 'dominance argument', the two games are entirely comparable, they are not so with respect to our present argument. In Game 2 the 'perfect judge argument' does not work since the judge has to arrive at his conclusion *before* he can observe whether $M will or will not have been given to our agent and for this he would have to be a predictor of human choices. The perfect judge in Game 1, however, needs no special powers except reasonable eyesight.

II

A further point I must now make is that by using our argument what can be shown is not merely that the predictor is not perfect but that he is devoid of all competence whatsoever! It is quite easy to prove that whatever the probability the predictor predicts that the player will take box II only, this probability cannot be any higher in the case where the player actually does take box II only, than in the case where he takes both boxes. For suppose the contrary, that the probability of the predictor predicting that the player takes box II only, if the player ends up taking both boxes, is only p, while if the player in fact takes box II only, it is $p + \epsilon$. (Note that if the predictor were infallible then p would equal zero and $\epsilon = 1$, but if he is not infallible yet competent to some degree, then $\epsilon > 0$.) Let the amount of money the predictor places in box II, if he predicts that the player will take box II only, be designated as x dollars rather than a million dollars. The expected desirability of choosing both boxes is $1000 + px$ dollars, since if the player takes both boxes he is sure to receive $1000 and there is a probability of p that in addition he also receives x dollars. The expected desirability of choosing box II only is, on the other hand $(p + \epsilon) x$ dollars. By making x sufficiently large ϵx can be made to exceed 1000 no matter how small ϵ is. The expected desirability of choosing box II only is higher than that of choosing both boxes and therefore it is in the player's best interest to choose box II only. But this is contrary to the opinion of the perfect judge and therefore we are forced to conclude that ϵ equals zero.

I should also like to mention that in the *British Journal for the Philosophy of Science* (1974), pp. 214–20, I have argued at some length that while there have been philosophers who have held that there are cases, i.e., communicated predictions, in which it is impossible to predict with certainty what a voluntary act will be, these are very special cases from which it may not be inferred that a normal voluntary act is unpredictable in principle. So as not to overtax the patience of the reader, who at this stage would still like some answers to more basic questions he may have concerning my whole approach (and whose worries I shall try my best to allay in the next two chapters), I shall not repeat my arguments here. I shall say only this: on a superficial look it may perhaps seem that in Game 1 too there is something special which we do not find in general in cases of free choices, namely that we can derive a contradiction if we assume that the predictor is competent. But surely this is not an argument *why* the prediction fails to be more successful but merely an argument *that* it fails to be so. The reason why predictors cannot be more reliably made apparently lies in the general nature of free human choices as I shall discuss later.

To conclude this chapter I shall summarize our findings so far by comparing Games 1 and 2. In Game 1 it is best to take both boxes, in Game 2, box II only. The difference arises out of the fact that in Game 1 it is a predictor who is offering $M on certain conditions whereas in Game 2 it is an observer. There are no obstacles for the observer to adhere strictly to his conditions to give the player $M if he takes box II only and to give him nothing if he takes both boxes. Since having $M is preferable to having $1000 only, obviously the player should take box II only. The predictor, on the other hand, is powerless to ensure that everything runs according to his conditions. He may predict that the player takes both boxes and hence not put anything in box II, yet the player happens to decide to take box II only and ends up with nothing; it is also possible that he predicts that the player takes box II only and thus put $M in it, yet in the end the player takes both boxes thus gaining $1 001 000. Since we do not believe in his power to predict, there is no reason to think that by taking both boxes it becomes more likely that there is no money in box II or that by taking box II only, the player renders it more probable that there is $M in it. Obviously therefore, the player should take both boxes, which contain more money than box II alone.

There are other differences as well between the two cases. In both cases we may construct hypothetical judges in whose opinion the player is better off by taking both boxes. In Game 1, to be rational, the player must accept the opinion of the relevant judge who is sufficiently well informed and whose advice it is therefore in his best interest to follow. In Game 2 however, we reject the advice of the kind of judge that may exist there on the grounds that he is not well informed. The judge in Game 1 must be well informed since the only relevant information he requires is whether there are or there are not a million dollars in box II and there are no obstacles preventing him from observing this. The judge in Game 2 on the other hand bases his advice on what he envisions the observer will later do. His information may not be reliable for if he 'sees' that the observer gives the player $M and the player follows his advice taking both boxes, it will, of necessity, turn out that, contrary to the 'vision' of our judge, the observer, who is in a solid position to ensure that he follows his own conditions, will give the player nothing.

In Game 1 however, even in those instances in which the player disregards the advice of the judge who sees with his own eyes the present state of box II and takes box II only, the predictor may fail to anticipate that he will do so. But one cannot cite any special reason why the predictor should have no competence in these instances. It seems, therefore, that the necessary failure of the predictor in these instances points to a fundamental aspect of voluntary choices, namely their unpredictability. In general, when I can choose between doing A or refraining from doing A and I am entirely unconstrained in my choice, in the sense (in which the strictest determinist agrees that sometimes I am unconstrained) that if for some reason I thought that doing A is preferable to not doing it then I can decide to do A, then a predictor will have no ability at all to predict what my choice is going to be. That is, it is not possible that a predictor will predict that I am going to do A with greater probability in case I actually end up doing A than in case I refrain from doing A. Because of their fundamental unpredictability, entirely voluntary choices may therefore be said to be free in a very radical sense, in a sense which will satisfy many theists who might otherwise be worried whether the human will was free in the requisite sense.

CHAPTER 14

SOME QUERIES CONCERNING THE ABSOLUTE INCOMPETENCE OF PREDICTORS

This chapter is devoted to the raising of questions against what has been said so far on the perfect incompetence of predictors. Each question, in my opinion, is one which thoughtful readers might themselves raise. In providing answers to all these questions, in the next chapter, through introducing a fundamental new feature of human choices of which no mention has yet been made I strongly believe we shall have gone a long way to clarify the issue before us.

(a) Some will have found it altogether objectionable that there be so much ado about such a highly remote and peculiar game in the context of the serious matters we are supposed to be dealing with here. They may feel that my whole case smacks of artificiality. In spite of the reassurances I tried to give in the previous chapter, they may remain convinced that it is by far too much and too soon to make generalizations about the unpredictability of all free choices on the basis of considering one strange instance.

(b) Virtually everyone will be prepared to admit that, should it ever be the case that the results of inductive and deductive logic clashed, then the former would have to give way to the latter. Now it seems that, on the evidence of the enormous past success of the predictor, inductive logic leads to the conclusion that it is best to take one of the boxes, while the 'perfect judge argument', which is allegedly a deductive argument, leads to the conclusion that it is best to take both boxes and therefore the latter conclusion must be correct. But how are we to explain now the fact that everybody who has arrived at the 'right' conclusion, that it is best to take both boxes, has ended up with less money than those who took the second box only? Of course, one may advance the suggestion that it was not competence at all but a mere incredibly fantastic coincidence that the predictor has never failed in the past. But such coincidences are incredibly unlikely to happen and, therefore, this explanation would be deemed too fantastic to be acceptable.

To make quite clear what this objection amounts to, consider the following: We are told by physicists that it is possible, though exceedingly improbable, that a heavy object in this room should spontaneously fly upwards. The reason is that there are billions of air molecules flying in all directions in this room and it could just happen that all the upward flying molecules congregated in one spot, namely below this heavy object, lifting it up. Such an event is to be expected to happen in this room once in every so many million years. Suppose a heavy object did suddenly fly upwards in this room. It might then be suggested that we need not look for possible external forces that might have been introduced to cause this to happen since such an event is bound to happen due to an extremely improbable configuration of the air molecules every so many million years and this was just such an occasion. It is quite clear that rather than accept this as the correct explanation we will try to discover another cause whose materialization is not so improbable. In general, we resist explanations which involve claiming that the extremely improbable has happened.

(c) The most difficult part of my claim to put up with is probably that reason demands that, even if we came across a predictor with a perfect record of one million successes, we should still regard him as perfectly incompetent, that is, as I have claimed to have shown on page 96 not only should we refuse to believe that he is a completely accomplished predictor but that he is even slightly competent. This seems clearly contrary to common experience. After all, any one without claiming to have hitherto unheard of powers can cite numerous examples, in which placing some of their friends with their familiar habits in a free choice situation, they would most probably correctly predict their actions. You can, perhaps, never claim to know with complete certainty what the choice of your intimate friend will be when asked — a question he has been asked a thousand times in your presence before — whether he prefers tea or coffee, yet your past experience renders your chances to anticipate his choice quite high.

(d) It may now also seem that we have proven much more than what we bargained for, so that as a result the theist is faced with a new difficulty.For suppose we raise the question, what if God himself took the place of the predictor? If our argument is sound, then it should seem to follow that even God could not anticipate what the choice of the player would be. But then what about God's omniscience?

Admittedly as we have explained in Part I God's omnipotence does not imply that he can do that which is logically impossible for him to do nor does his omniscience imply that he knows that which it is logically impossible for him to know. And according to our argument, it may be logically impossible for God to grant the player complete freedom to choose exactly as he pleases and ensure at the same time that he can predict what he will choose. Yet, while it is also known that in the past a number of philosophers have held that an omniscient God is not required to be able to predict a free human act, these philosophers did not feel impelled to go to the extreme and claim that God is an absolutely incompetent predictor, i.e., that he cannot correctly predict any human act with appreciable probability. Consequently, it is not impossible to envisage that God is able to ensure that the world is conducted according to various Divine plans. Suppose God desires that an act A is done to an individual X at time t. He then sees to it that person Y is around at the appropriate time, of whom God knows that it is highly probable that he will perform A on X. On those rare occasions on which the improbable happens and Y is not prepared to perform A freely, perhaps God interferes with his freedom and makes him perform A anyhow. In this way, one can reconcile the fact that God is not wholly omniscient where free human acts are concerned, with the fact that it is he who guides history along lines he wishes and, at the same time, leaving human freedom largely intact. But if we are forced to maintain, as it would seem to be the case from what we said before, that God has no competence whatever in predicting free human acts, then it is hard to see how he manages the world so as to achieve all the Divine goals he has set for humanity without depriving men of their freedom much of the time.

(e) Had we defined 'free choice' as a choice which can, in principle, not be predicted, then it would indeed clearly be, in principle, impossible to predict free choices. But to the agent in our story we assign freedom of choice only in the sense that he acts exactly as he deems fit and not against his will, without making unpredictability a part of the definition of free will. Consequently, it does not seem at all incoherent to claim that his choices should be predictable. How can one insist that a perfect predictor or that even just a somewhat competent predictor is, in principle, impossible?

(f) Professors R. Brier and W. Walther have pointed out that the perfect judge's intelligence is no less inductively established than the competence of the predictor and we are still left with a choice between scrapping the predictor or the perfect judge.[1] They also claim that it may be risky to rely on the opinion of our judge. Our judge may think that he sees money in box II and be of the opinion that the agent might as well go ahead and take both boxes. However, should he indeed do so he would find box II empty, and our judge would discover he had made a mistake, his eyes had played tricks on him.

(g) Our argument from the perfect judge was based on the assumption that if the predictor is competent then the introduction of a third person, who is not communicating to the agent what he sees, cannot, surely, interfere with his powers of predic-

---

[1] 'Newcomb's Paradox' (unpublished paper).

tion. But perhaps it could be maintained that the predictor is competent or even perfect, but he loses his powers altogether — for reasons which of course we do not know — if you allow any person to observe the contents of box II.

(h) Why must the contradiction we have arrived at be taken as indicating that our assumption, that it is possible to have a competent predictor, has to be withdrawn? Why could we not retain our belief that a perfect predictor, as such might, in principle, exist, and merely conclude that what is impossible is that he could interact with those whose free choices he is predicting. That is, he loses his powers if he sets up choices for those whose actions he is to predict?

CHAPTER 15

THE PREDICTOR AS A DIAGNOSTICIAN

I

In order to really illuminate what is going on we shall introduce a variation on Game 1. We shall not be dealing with someone who gives even the slightest impression that he is a precognitor looking directly into the future or is a Laplacean Demon who knows all the laws of nature and initial conditions; but all that we shall postulate is an expert on the electric stimulation of the brain, who at t_0 places a helmet, from which a number of electrodes are protruding, upon the head of the agent. The helmet is connected to a complicated electrical apparatus equipped with two buttons. If the experimenter pushes button 1 (i.e., does B_1), then a complex pattern of electric current flows into the various parts of the agent's brain and causes him to want to do C_1 at t_1, while if he presses button 2 (i.e., does B_2) then a different pattern results which definitely causes him to do C_2. As in the other game, if P_1 results, the experimenter puts \$M into box II and if P_2 results, he puts nothing into box II. Let us assume that the experimenter has performed his experiment one million times, in 500 000 cases doing B_1, in 500 000 doing B_2. Now in all those cases which he did B_1, the various agents involved here for all sorts of imaginable and different reasons decided to do C_1, whereas in other cases, for thousands of different reasons, they did C_2. Let us imagine that we are confronted with player number one million and one who at t_0 had the helmet placed on his head but has no idea which button the experimenter has pushed and is asking us for advice about what he should do at t_1 in order to maximize the amount of money gained. I am sure that no one will wish to dispute that if we feel there is any point in advising him then we shall regard the fact that all those who in the past did C_2 had ended up with less money than anyone who did C_1 as entirely irrelevant. We know that those who did C_1 did so because they were caused to do so by the experimenter and if any one of them had been capable of breaking loose from the influence of B_1 and had managed to do C_2, he would have definitely ended up with \$1 001 000; while any one for whom B_2 was the case, box II was left empty; and if he would have, through an extraordinary exertion of will, done C_1, he would have ended up with no money at all. We realize that, clearly the causal connection is not between B_1 and C_1 or between B_2 and C_2, but that B_1 merely causes a very strong tendency to do C_1 and hitherto all those who had a strong tendency to do C_1 ended up doing C_1. Thus, in the case where, for our agent, it is a fact that B_1, then the brain specialist is sure to have money in box II, and if the agent should, somehow by the exercise of will, act contrary to his tendency and end up doing C_2 this is not going to change B_1 and P_1, and he will be getting an extra \$1000. It may, of course, well be the case that if B_1 occurs, then no matter what we say, the agent will do C_1, yet we shall go on advising that he should by all means try doing C_2.

Now we may return to the original Newcomb's game realizing that it is possible to assess differently the significance of the evidence provided by the predictor's past record. He may not have any direct access to the final choices of the agent. Instead, what he may be able to do perfectly well is to identify the physical causes which are already present at t_0 and which tend to compel the predictor to make his particular choice. Hitherto, every player ended up acting at t_1 in accordance with the tendency he had at t_0 to act. Suppose the causal situation at t_0 in the case of our agent is the kind which is always associated with the agent doing C_1 at t_1, then the predictor unfailingly recognizes this and does P_1. It may well be that in this case no matter how strongly we urge the agent to do C_2, he just will not do it, we should still of course insist that it is best for him to do C_2. By actually ending up doing C_2 he is not going to bring about P_2, that box II is empty, but he only gains an extra thousand dollars.

Here we have encountered then the manifestation of a very important aspect of confirmation theory which is that a particular experience as such cannot, on its own, be said either to confirm or not to confirm a given hypothesis. The question of whether or not a given set of observations confirms a given hypothesis depends on the theories we subscribe to or on the prior assumption we already hold. In the light of our new theory proposed here, for instance, choices are strongly determined by tendencies which may, in turn, be determined by prior causes, but these prior causes are only indirectly connected with the final choices. Consequently, the enormous past success of the predictor is not attributed to sheer coincidence but to a genuine power; however, it is the kind of power which does not provide any reason for the agent to fear that by doing C_2 he may be jeopardizing his chances of discovering money in box II. One may find this new theory attractive enough to want to adopt it without being under any pressure to adopt it. The point is, however, that after being presented with the 'perfect judge argument', which prevents us from believing that C_1 is the best choice, we are actually forced to abandon the theory according to which any change in the final choice necessarily entails a change in the original prediction, and subscribe to the new theory which views the predictor less as a predictor and rather as a perfect diagnostician of tendencies.

To present what has been said slightly more formally, let

T_1 = The agent has the tendency to do C_1
T_2 = The agent has the tendency to do C_2
D_1 = The Predictor diagnoses that T_1
D_2 = The Predictor diagnoses that T_2.

Now the outstanding, perfect record of successes of our so-called 'predictor' may be interpreted as showing that he is a

perfect diagnostician of tendencies and at t_0 can, without fail, recognize the tendency the agent has to choose at t_1.
Thus

$$T_1 \equiv D_1$$

which means that 'If and only if the agent has the tendency to end up choosing box II only, then the 'predictor' diagnoses that he has the tendency to end up choosing box II only'.
Similarly

$$T_2 \equiv D_2.$$

Also

$$D_1 \equiv P_1 \quad \text{and} \quad D_2 \equiv P_2$$

which, of course, means that the 'predictor' always bases his prediction on his diagnosis. From this it follows that

$$T_1 \equiv P_1 \ldots (\alpha) \quad \text{and} \quad T_2 \equiv P_2 \ldots (\alpha').$$

It is consistent with everything said so far to maintain that

$$p(C_1/T_1) = p(C_2/T_2) = 0.99\ldots.99$$

i.e., that the probability of the agent doing C_i, when it is a fact that T_i, is extremely high; the vast majority of people having the tendency of taking only one of the boxes, for instance, do actually end up doing so. Also, of course

$$P(C_1/T_2) = p(C_2/T_1) = 0.00\ldots.01$$

because, indeed, very few people act contrary to their tendency. In passing it should be mentioned that of those players who, during the first 29 minutes and 59 seconds of the half hour allotted to them for deliberation, are determined to do C_1 and only in the last second change their mind and end up doing C_2, it is also true in the vast majority of cases that T_2.

Any player who ever played or will ever play the game will be assumed to be in one of the following classes:

	T_1	T_2
C_1	(a) very large $p(P_1) = 1$	(c) very small $p(P_1) = 0$
C_2	(b) very small $p(P_1) = 1$	(d) very large $p(P_1) = 0$

Since class a is much larger than class c, then if all we are given is that an agent is in a class characterized by C_1, then he is much more likely to be in a than in c, or characterized by T_1 than by T_2, or (because of (α) and (α')) by P_1 rather than P_2. And when all we have is that the agent is in class C_2, then he is much more likely to be in d than in b. It follows therefore that

$$p(T_1/C_1) \gg p(T_2/C_1) \text{ and } p(T_2/C_2) \gg p(T_1/C_2)$$

which amounts — because of (α) and (α') — to

$$p(P_1/C_1) \gg p(P_2/C_1) \text{ and } p(P_2/C_2) \gg p(P_1/C_2) \dots (\beta).$$

Thus, the probability that the 'predictor' will make the prediction that C_i, is vastly greater than that he will make the prediction C_j, if it is in fact C_i.

It is also obvious now that if it is the case that the agent is in the class characterized by T_2, then by going against his tendency and choosing box II only, all he can do is transfer himself from d to c, which is of no use to him at all since the predictor will still predict that C_2. Thus he will give up the $1000 of box I without increasing his chances in the slightest to receive $M. Also, if it is a fact that he is in a class characterized by T_1, then by actually doing C_2 he does not, in the least, jeopardize his chances to get the $M and he can only gain $1000 by transferring himself from a to b.

II

The basis for Objection (b) of the last chapter has, of course, disappeared. We no longer resolve the contradiction that it is, on the one hand (because of the established competence of the predictor), best to do C_1 and, on the other, it is (because of the advice of the well-wisher) best to do C_2, by ignoring inductive evidence. What I suggest, instead, is that it is possible to reinterpret this evidence by adopting a particular view of human nature. The perfect record of the 'predictor' is not put down as an incredible coincidence but is taken as evidence that he is a perfect diagnostician. It is only indirectly, because of the extremely high correlation between T_i and C_i, that he is a predictor at all.

Nothing remains of Objection (c) either. Of course, we are very often able to predict how our friends are going to act in a free-choice situation. We ourselves are pretty good diagnosticians of the tendencies of some people. But, of course, there is nothing to fear from the 'predictor' in our game, who happens to be a perfect diagnostician, in spite of (β). Whether or not the agent will find money in box II depends entirely on the tendency he is carrying in him and he can quite safely decide to pick both boxes and make sure he does not lose the $1000 which is in box I.

Incidentally, there is, in general, nothing to fear from any predictor — be he even an omniscient predictor — who proposes to punish us at t_0, if and only if, we perform an act A at a later time t_1 — the punishment becoming known to us only after t_1. It could, of course, very well be the case that he predicts with extremely high probability whether or not we will do A at t_1. Yet there is no point for us to refrain from doing A should we desire it. The predictor can, at most, have full access to our tendencies but our actual choice does not affect his prediction.

Now we can turn our attention to the objection raised under (a). First of all it should be mentioned that Newcomb's peculiar story concerning his game is, of course, merely one instance of indefinitely many stories one might construct involving arrangements featuring a predictor of choices, which would lead to a contradiction. The required arrangement is one where a predictor wishes to reward us in advance for doing what, in the opinion of an independent observer, ultimately leads to less reward than an alternative action and we are in a situation to work out with certainty the opinion of the observer.

But a more important point is this. By introducing our story concerning the expert on the electric stimulation of the brain and consequently the possibility of explaining the past success of any predictor as due to his excellence as a diagnostician of tendencies, it has been demonstrated that, in principle, there can be no evidence for the existence of a competent predictor *qua* predictor; that is, one whose prediction is directly connected to the final choice. For this conclusion we do not rely in any way on the contradiction derived from the specific story of Game 1.

The worry expressed in (d) obviously disappears too. When it is claimed that all predictors must be entirely incompetent this means only that the agent has not got the least reason to fear that, by deciding to make a given choice at t_1, he may bring about or even just slightly raise the probability that the predictor has performed a given act at t_0, before t_1. Yet, as we have shown, this is entirely compatible with the assertion that $p(P_1/C_1) \gg p(P_1/C_2)$, i.e., that the probability that the predictor makes a correct prediction of the agent's choice is much higher than that he will predict wrongly. There is no reason not to suppose that God is able to foresee with exceedingly high probability what free human choices will be. He certainly should be assumed to be a perfect diagnostician of human tendencies.

It may be of some interest to note that perhaps I could claim Biblical support for the view just expressed. The prophet Jonah is commanded to go and announce to the people of Nineveh — what he finally agrees to do as described in Chapter 3 v. 4 — 'Yet forty days and Nineveh shall be overthrown.' As we know he is initially reluctant to do this, for the reason — which later becomes apparent — of being afraid of the embarassment he might suffer if his prophecy should turn out to be false in the event that the people of Nineveh should repent. It was apparently established that their tendency was definitely not to repent and that is why he was to make the categorical assertion that their city will be destroyed. However, Jonah realized that through their exertion of free will the unexpected might happen and the people of Nineveh decide to mend their ways.[1]

As to Objection (e), it could, of course, have been replied that it is an altogether illegitimate objection. After all, when in geometry we prove, for instance, that any triangle in which two angles are equal is an isosceles triangle by demonstrating that on the assumption of the denial of this claim we are led to an absurdity (i.e., to the denial of a theorem already proven before), our proof of the impossibility of a non-isosceles triangle in which two angles are equal is unquestioned. To query this proof by pointing out that there seems to be nothing incoherent in the statement "There is a triangle in which all the sides are of a different length though two of its angles are equal", is to misunderstand the nature of a *reductio ad absurdum* proof. Similarly here, if it is demonstrated that the assumption of the existence of a competent predictor leads to the contradiction that it is both best to do C_1 and C_2, then the falsity of this assumption is established (unless, of course, in the demonstration we made use of some other assumptions as well, the truth of which may be questioned).

Yet it could be countered that there is a difference between proving that something is the case and making us see why it should be the case. In other words, it is not entirely improper, after having been shown that the 'predictor' may be completely ignored despite his phenomenal record, to request the illumination of the factor which is responsible for this unexpected result. Now we have achieved the sought-after insight. Freely willed choices are

---

[1] Any one worried that because of the timelessness of God, he must always know what happens at any time, should consult Nelson Pike's *God and Timelessness* (London, 1970) where he seriously questions the coherence of the notion of timelessness.

inaccessible to prior discernment, although they can indirectly be guessed correctly with near certainty via the tendencies imprinted in the brains of the agents.

At this point I should like to introduce one more argument why the kind of predictor featuring in Game 1 cannot be proficient. Yet one more argument in support of this contention can only serve to reassure us that the line pursued here is sound. The argument involves a very fundamental aspect of the nature of time and I can afford to do no more than merely touch the surface of a very complex issue.

In the course of his extensive analysis[2] of the concept of causality von Wright says this:

I now propose the following way of distinguishing between cause and effect by the means of action: p is a cause relative to q and q an effect relative to p if and only if by doing p we could bring about q or by suppressing p we could remove q or prevent it from happening.

Many of those who would not fully go along with Von Wright's definition may still agree that here, where C_i may be done by the agent with the intention of securing P_i and where the agent is free to contemplate and decide what situation he would like at t_0 to have obtained and acts accordingly at t_1, it is his action that should be regarded as the cause. The predictor on the other hand, if he is to be assumed proficient, seems to *depend* for his prediction on the decision of the agent and therefore it is proper to deem P_i as the effect. In that case we would be facing here an instance of backward causation. But it may be contended that there are grounds for saying that backward causation is, in principle, impossible.

The reason — which I shall indicate very briefly — why events of the future may not be capable of influencing the present, may be the unreality of the future. The unreality of the future, as opposed to the reality of the past, has been maintained by different philo-

----

[2] *Explanation and Understanding*, London, 1971, pp. 70–81.

sophers in different ways. Everyone has, of course, realized that neither the events of the past nor those of the future occur in the present, however what has been said is that the former having actually occurred do not cease to be real, while the latter which are to become real later only, are as yet unreal. In a well known passage, C. D. Broad says:

'The sum of total existence is always increasing, and it is this which given the time-series a sense as well as an order. A moment t is later than a moment t' if the sum total of existence at t includes the sum total of existence at t' together with something more.'[3]

Thus the events of the past, but not those of the future, have an existence in the present. This idea when carried to its extreme leads to the view that propositions concerning future contingencies have no truth-value at all and one cannot refer to particular future events as they are not there to be referred to. But even those who are not embracing the most extreme position in denying the reality of the future may still claim that events not having yet occurred lack existence to be able to exert an influence upon the present state of affairs. There are philosophers who, while not necessarily going as far as to claim that sentences referring to future events are altogether devoid of meaning, hold that, to believe that an event not yet materialized might be capable of bringing forth any effects in the actual world, is comparable, for example, to believing illogically, that a non-existent object may occupy a given position in real space. It is only past events, whose existence has not ceased, that are capable of shaping our world now, but the events of the future, are not there yet to reach out into the present so as to affect it.

As to Objection (f), had I not introduced the distinction just discussed between what is and what is not accessible for discernment at t_0 in the context of an act of free choice at a later time t_1, my answer would have had to run along the following lines.

[3] *Scientific Thought* (1952), pp. 66–7.

Indeed my proof of the impossibility of a competent predictor was a *reductio ad absurdum* proof only; we were told a story and the story led to a contradiction from which all we know is that our story must have included some impossible element. (I would have to admit that it is not entirely unambiguously given which element of our story is the impossible one.) But when it comes to a choice between rejecting the assumption that one is capable of establishing that someone is fairly intelligent and sees what he thinks he sees or whether a predictor, as required in our game, exists, it may be safely said that virtually everyone would give up the latter assumption. A not too good reason why this should be so is that people who can perform what the perfect judge in our story performs, are widely believed to have actually existed while Newcomb's predictor is not ever claimed to have been encountered in real life. Brier and Walther could justifiably object to this and say, what if such people, too, were everyday phenomena? A better reason would be that the denial of the possibility of ever establishing with scientific certainty that someone is as minimally intelligent as it is required for our judge to be and can see what is in front of him, would work far more havoc with our whole system of knowledge than the denial of the possibility of predicting human choices.

But now, of course, an even better reason may be offered. To deny that it is possible for someone to play the role of the judge in our story would be flying in the face of every strong inductive evidence. But under no circumstances can there be real evidence that a predictor, who needs to be feared when making our choices, exists. No matter what the alleged evidence, it may always be reinterpreted along the lines drawn here.

The answer to Objection (g) is very similar. That someone should under normal circumstances be a perfect predictor of free choices but completely lose his power when an entirely innocuous observer is introduced, would seem very strange and inexplicable. But we have already provided adequate reasons why no one in general is an effective predictor of choices.

The answer to Objection (h) is of course first of all, that there does not seem to be a good explanation why, if our predictor is wholly efficacious as such, he should become incapacitated by his setting up choices for those whose actions he is to predict. In addition no explanation whatever could be offered to account for the enormous past success of the predictor who was interacting with all the players whose choices he did not fail to predict.

Finally, a most important point: In order to derive that C_2 is the best choice we did not really need to introduce a third person to serve as our perfect judge. The predictor himself could serve that function! The agent can be absolutely certain that the predictor, who is indisputably in a perfect position to know, is of the opinion that it is best to do C_2. In particular, suppose the predictor has already put $M in box II and he asks himself what choice would be the best for the agent to do. Then his thoughts would surely run along these lines: of course (given that I am a perfect predictor) the agent cannot but do C_1, however (given that under no circumstances am I going to make the money disappear from box II) theoretically speaking, in the present context, he would certainly be better off doing C_2. Using the predictor as our perfect judge simplifies matters in general; in particular it renders it impossible to raise Objections (f) and (g) in the first place.

III

We began Part II of this book by pointing out that there is a seeming conflict between science and religion concerning the matter of free will. In other words theism seemed to be to a certain degree disconfirmed by all those scientific results which have been taken as supporting the doctrine that all events are in principle predictable. It is of crucial importance to realize that what we have done in the last few chapters amounts to more than just eliminating a threat of disconfirmation. What we actually have now is a positive confirmation to some degree of the credibility of theism.

Part III will be devoted to a more thorough explanation of the nature of empirical confirmation, but because of the vital need to gain a correct understanding of this matter I permit myself to make here some preliminary remarks. We have seen that quite a number of theists thought it essential to maintain that some human choices are unpredictable, even by an omniscient being. Even more theists hold that humans must be — for the sake of the possibility to be held responsible for some of their action — free at least to the extent that not all their action can be predicted on the basis of all the initial conditions and laws of nature. We have claimed that this can be shown to be the case. It is easily imaginable that human nature was different and all human choices were, in principle, predictable. (Such a situation would obtain if humans acted in accordance with a number of known rules irrespective of their wishes, that is, they were often compelled to act contrary to their wishes.) For this reason we cannot but regard the fact that human nature happens to be the way it is as amounting to actual confirmation of theism.

In view of the fact that there is so much misapprehension surrounding this issue I had better explain. Renford Bambrough forcefully expresses a sentiment which is very common among contemporary philosophers — a sentiment I shall have opportunity to discuss later at length — when he says:

Is it conceivable that God should exist and yet that everything else should remain exactly the same as if he did not exist? Is it conceivable that God should not exist and yet that everything else should remain the same as if he did exist?[4]

In my opinion, he is asking a highly pertinent question and is absolutely right in implying that theism can have no substance if it indeed were the case that it made no difference to the world we lived in, whether there is or there is no God. But of course,

---

[4] *Reason, Truth and God* (London, 1969) p. 52.

God's existence makes a great deal of difference. One we have just seen is that: if Naturalism were true, that is, there was no God, then there would have been absolutely no reason why human nature should be as it happens to be; Naturalism permits the complete predictability of all human actions. If, however, theism is true then human nature just could not be different in this essential respect from what we now know it is.[5]

Now even at this preliminary stage I have to forestall an objection an unsympathetic reader is quite likely to raise: there are many naturalists who deny the predictability of free choices; how then can I state categorically that naturalists permit the predictability of choices? I take however Naturalism and theism as two competing views concerning the question what lies behind the physical universe and as being entirely confined to answering this question. According to Naturalism the answer is nothing. All the properties of the universe are what they are and it makes no sense to ask, why or who willed them to be so. To the theist, on the other hand, this is a most important question and the answer is: the universe and all its properties are the result of the will of a Perfect Being.

Thus naturalists may hold all sorts of theories concerning the nature of human beings: that they are entirely free agents or no better than mere robots, etc. but *qua* naturalists they are not even committed to the view that there are any laws which render any kind of events predictable. The only definite view that Naturalism imposes upon its supporters is that nothing exists apart from the physical universe. On the other hand, the theory the theist holds concerning the origins of the universe, is sufficient in itself to commit him to a large number of views on what sorts of thing we must find in the universe. Since benevolence contributes to

[5] While Naturalism and Theism may be the major candidates for an answer to the question what is behind the universe, there are indefinitely many others as well. In Part III I shall be dealing with this problem.

perfection, a Perfect Being must be Omnibenevolent. It is not unreasonable to hold that an Omnibenevolent Being should wish that a special kind of creature should exist who can add to the goodness of the world by introducing into it the unique virtue that results when a creature, who is subject to temptation, exercises his free will to overcome his evil impulses.

One need not have great expert knowledge of scientific methodology to appreciate that, in general, a state of affairs confirms a hypothesis relative to its rival if the hypothesis in question requires that the given state of affairs obtains while its rival does not require it. What we mean when we say that a hypothesis is confirmed by a given state of affairs relative to its rival is, that the relative credibility of the hypothesis is greater in virtue of the presence of the aforesaid state of affairs from what it would be in its absence. We say nothing yet about degrees of confirmation or the amount of confirmation required to make a hypothesis acceptable. The relevant state of affairs in our case is the way humans happen to be constructed possessing the radical kind of freedom we have shown they possess. Theism requires — on some interpretations at least — that this is so. If this were not so Theism would have been disconfirmed to a considerable degree. The fact that things are the way they are must be admitted bestows a certain amount of confirmation upon Theism.

α-MACHINES AND β-MACHINES

I

According to the religious world view, a human being occupies a specially elevated position in the order of creation. He is supposed to have been created in the image of God, which of course, does not mean that any part of his body has been fashioned to resemble God's but that he has been endowed with something special — characteristic of the Divine — a mind. This spark of God, which is in him, transforms him from a mere material system into a spiritual being.

If it could be shown that, by virtue of having a mind, a person is superior to a mindless machine in some tangible and significant way, many would find that this would enhance the status of minded beings and strengthen the position of the Theist *vis-à-vis* the Naturalist. The latter has no reason to believe that having a mind carries with it extraordinary capacities. He is not prevented from holding that an admittedly mindless machine might outstrip a minded man in every sphere of performance we regard worthy of admiration.

One noted effort to claim that there is a basic difference between the abilities of men and machines was made by J. R. Lucas.[1] The area in which he thought human competence exceeds that of an artificial intelligence is in logic and mathematics, or in general, in deductive reasoning or theorem-proving. In spite of the fact that this is the very area in which computers have made their most impressive advances, Lucas believes that they are ultimately

[1] 'Minds, Machines & Gödel', *Philosophy* (1961), pp. 112—27.

limited in a way in which people are not. In his view, for every machine there are theorems which it cannot, in principle, prove, while humans, due to their self-consciousness, can be assumed to be able — at least in principle — to prove any theorem. His argument, however, has not enjoyed general acceptance. Some have thought that he has not conclusively shown that for every machine there are theorems which are beyond its capacity to prove. But even if his arguments were sufficient to prove this, he has certainly done very little to provide a rigorous proof that, with the possession of a mind and consciousness, one necessarily overcomes any such limitations. Indeed, it would have been most surprising if he could have succeeded in convincingly showing in a relatively short article, that computers can be beaten at their own game; that in the most unlikely domain of deductive reasoning, which is their forte, computers can be outdone by humans.

I propose to defend the view that minded systems are specially privileged systems, but shall not claim that this privilege necessarily consists of some special skill or ability. I shall attempt to show that there is a basic difference between men and machines in that a certain kind of freedom is enjoyed by the former and not by the latter. The freedom of men I am referring to is what we have just discovered to exist, namely that certain human acts are, in principle, unpredictable. I shall attempt to show that this unpredictability is intimately connected with the fact that humans possess mental properties. Now of course, everyone agrees that in a certain sense people have freedom that mindless machines cannot have. Human beings can sometimes do exactly what they want in contrast to a mindless machine, of which it can never be said that it does what it wants, since in order to want anything it would need to have a mind. But saying this, of course, adds absolutely nothing to saying that mindless systems are mindless. What I want to show, however, is that the admitted difference between the two systems leads to another, quite unexpected difference. I shall argue that the possession of a mind implies the

unpredictability of some of the acts of a mind possessor, an unpredictability which does not apply to mindless systems.

II

We have already had opportunity to refer to the essential unpredictability of some human acts that have been discussed by other
philosophers. It has been pointed out[2] that a human being who is
determined to act counterpredictively, cannot have his actions
predicted and also have the prediction communicated to him. The
communicated prediction is assured not to come true by virtue of
the fact that the counterpredictively-motivated person, having
learnt how he is supposed to act, will decide to act differently.
This kind of unpredictability does not, however, seem to be
connected with the humanity of man. A machine programmed to
act counterpredictively would also act in a way which would make
communicated predictions impossible. In order to show that men
are different (which by the way was not the aim of these philosophers) it would have to be proven that machines cannot be
counterpredictively programmed.

I shall be discussing the kind of unpredictability which we have
shown to exist with respect to a player in Game 1. To begin our
inquiries we shall consider what happens when all the conditions
are kept the same as before except that the human player is
replaced by a machine. Let us first suppose that our player is a
machine of type α which is programmed to always take box II
only. There are clearly no difficulties for our predictor here; he
can observe his rules and successfully predict that α will take box
II only. No contradiction arises here. To the question would α be
better off if it took both boxes? the answer is, yes. If it took both
boxes it would get \$1 001 000, but of course it cannot take both
boxes since it is an α-machine. There is no contrary conclusion

---

[2] e.g., M. Scriven, 'An Essential Unpredictability of Human Behavior'.

based on inductive evidence; past happenings cannot be construed as evidence that if it took both boxes it would end up with less money. The reason being that no α-machine has ever taken both boxes and ended up with only $1000, since no α-machine has ever taken both boxes. After all, the infallibility of the predictor with respect to the choices of α-machine, derives from the fact that α-machines can always be relied on taking box II only. If something should go wrong and an α-machine were to take both boxes the predictor would not know this. We can therefore, find nothing in our past observations which could be construed as evidence for the truth of the counter-factual 'If this α-machine would have taken both boxes it would have found the second box empty.'

Now let the player be a β-machine which is programmed always to take both boxes. The predictor can once more adhere to his rules and predict with perfect confidence that β will pick both boxes and hence leave box II empty. No contradiction arises here either. To the question had β been better off if it picked box II only? there is only one answer: no. If it had picked box II only, it would have ended up with nothing. No contrary claim could be advanced on the basis of the predictor's principle to always reward those who are content with taking box II alone by a million dollars. No β-machine ever takes box II alone and is rewarded with a million dollars, since no β-machine ever takes box II alone. There is nothing which would support the truth of the counter-factual 'If this β-machine would have taken box II only it would have a million dollars in it.' The reason why the predictor has been infallible with respect to the choices of β-machines is because these machines could be relied upon to pick both boxes. There is no basis to believe that if something so extraordinary happened that a β-machine took box II only, the predictor would be able to predict this.

Now the following question may seem to arise: Having free will means only having the ability to act in accordance with one's will; a free agent is not constrained to act against his will but does exactly what he wants. I certainly do not wish to define a free agent as one who is necessarily undetermined or unprogrammed to will what he is going to will (otherwise the unpredictability of the choices of a free-willed agent would be established by fiat, whereas I claim it interestingly follows from the argument of the previous chapters. Thus it does not seem illegitimate to claim that the human agent, presently facing the choices of Game 1, is determined (or programmed) to will either to choose box II only or to will to choose to take both boxes. But then, in essence, our human agent is either like an α-machine or like a β-machine and we have just shown that in either case it can be maintained without fear of contradiction that the predictor is infallible.

The answer to this is that while it might be maintained that the choice of the agent is predetermined and while it is undoubtedly true that he must either choose to take box II only or both boxes, it does not follow that the agent must be either in an α-state, in which case the same argument which applied to α-machines applies to him, or if not then in a β-state in which case the same argument which applied to β-machines applies to him. For suppose he makes the choice of taking both boxes. Can we really say that he may be treated in every respect as a β-machine? It does not seem so. For consider the question 'Would he have been better off if he had taken only box II?' From the perfect judge argument the answer which follows is, no. But on the assumption that the predictor is infallible, there is also a contrary answer, namely, that if he only took box II there would have been $M in it and thus he would have gained more. The rebuttal we had in the case of β-machines, that there is no evidential basis for saying that anybody in a similar state to our present player, who has taken box II, was only rewarded by $M since no-one in a similar state to our present player ever took box II only, is not available here. Before our human player made his decision he was free to make his choice according to what he thought was best for him and in this he is very much unlike a β-machine, who must choose both boxes. Had

he thought he would benefit more by taking box II only, then
most probably, he would have taken box II only. But then he
would have gained a million dollars because everybody in the past
who thought it is better to take box II only and took box II only,
received a million dollars. Hence we have a contradiction and are
forced to conclude that the predictor is not infallible.

γ-MACHINES AND δ-MACHINES

I

It would seem therefore, that a human player resembles more a γ-machine which is programmed to employ logic, both deductive and inductive and on the basis of empirical evidence figure out which choice will maximize its gain and make that choice. How will such a machine act? Assuming that our argument from the perfect judge is correct it should reason that taking both boxes will result in the highest amount of money to be gained and thus take both boxes. The predictor may know all this and hence predict correctly that the γ-machine is going to take both boxes and thus leave box II empty. But does not a contradiction arise here as well? Is there no argument for also saying that the machine would gain more by picking box II only? The answer is that there is no evidential support for the truth of the counter-factual 'If this γ-machine would have taken box II only it would have found $M in it', since no γ-machine has ever taken box II only and gained $M simply because no γ-machine has ever taken box II only. The very reason why the predictor is infallible, with respect to the choices of a γ-machine, is because the γ-machine can be relied upon to take both boxes.

From what has just been said it may appear that one could advance an argument to the effect that maintaining that a perfect predictor with respect to the choices of a human player may exist, does not lead to a contradiction either. For suppose, as we have already supposed, that our human player wants to maximize his gain. Then he is, in essence, a γ-machine. Then because of the argument from the perfect well-wisher he must choose to take both boxes. There is no argument, so it might be claimed, which leads to the contrary conclusion, that he would be better off by taking box II only. True enough, every player who takes box II only, gains a million dollars while every player who takes both boxes gets only a thousand dollars, but nobody who is a player and is in a γ-state and who takes box II only, gains a million dollars, simply because nobody who is in a γ-state takes box II only. There is no evidential support for the truth of the counterfactual 'If this player, who is in γ-state, had taken box II only he would have gained \$M.'

There is a very fundamental difference, however, between the human-player and the computer player. In the case of the human being it makes full sense to say that, though he wants to do an act which achieves a given aim, he actually performs a different act. Of a non-minded machine one can of course not say this. Consequently the many thousands of people who, in the past games, have chosen to take box II only, may well include many who were in γ-state, that is, they were desirous to maximize their gains, yet took box II only. Therefore, the present agent who wants to maximize his gain does have good grounds for arguing that if he had taken box II only he would have been better off than he is by taking both boxes, since in the past, people who were in a γ-state like himself and took box II only, ended up with a million dollars, while those who took both boxes got only a thousand.

Thus, man's possession of mental properties, by virtue of which he may want to perform an act designated by logic, as the act securing the best results but actually performs a different act, is the crucial factor in rendering the predictor ineffectual. In the case of the machine which has no wants, there is no contradiction in maintaining that the predictor is infallible with respect to his choices and the best thing is to take both boxes, since no other argument exists for saying that it would be better off taking box II only. In the case of the human agent there is such an argument.

Hence, a contradiction, and we must conclude that a reliable predictor with respect to his choices, cannot exist.

An attempt could be conceivably made to defend the claim that an argument for saying that the player would be better off by taking box II only, lacks in the case of the human agent, too. All those people in the past who have wanted to maximize their gain yet took box II only, evidently did not appreciate the argument from the advice of the perfect judge, which logically implies that in order to achieve their goal they would have to take both boxes. The present agent, however, realizes this. Thus he cannot argue that if he had taken box II only he would have been better off on the basis that everyone with a state of mind like his, who took box II only, found a million dollars in it. The reason is that nobody who was in a similar state of mind as the present agent — that is, who was both desirous to maximize his gain and was aware of the deductive argument for taking both boxes — had ever taken box II in the past and found a million dollars in it, simply because no such person has chosen to take box II only. What we are saying then is, that γ splits up into γ_1, and γ_2. A player is in γ_1-state if he desires to maximize his gain but does not realize that, in order to do so, logic requires that he should be taking both boxes; a player is in γ_2-state if he desires to maximize his gain and realizes that, in order to do so, logic requires that he should take both boxes. Our present player is in γ_2-state. He has no evidential basis for the truth of the counterfactual 'If I (who am in γ_2-state) would have taken box II only, I would have gained \$M', since no one in γ_2-state ever took box II only.

But the erroneous assumption underlying such an attempt is that a human agent, who is aware of the deductive argument for taking both boxes, will not ever choose to take box II only. It is easily imaginable that an agent strongly desirous to gain the maximum amount of money and aware of the argument that a perfect well-wisher, who could observe the contents of box II, would certainly advise him to take both boxes, yet decides to take box II only. He might end up doing so for any number of reasons. For example, he may decide (fallaciously) that this argument does not, after all, lead to the conclusion that he would be better off taking both boxes, or that logic is not a reliable guide in practical matters. Most importantly, he may decide to take box II only, without feeling obliged to give a rational defense — even to himself — for his choice. Therefore the sample class of the present agent may contain past players who were bent upon maximizing their gain and were aware of the deductive argument for taking both boxes but have decided not to pay attention to it and took box II only, ending up with a million dollars. Thus on the assumption that the predictor is reliable, the present player has solid evidence for maintaining that he would have been better off if he had taken box II only. He is entitled to maintain the generalization: everybody, who like himself, was in γ_2-state wanting to maximize his gain and being aware of the argument for taking both boxes, yet decides to ignore that argument and takes box II only, gains a million dollars, while those who do pay attention to that argument and go for both boxes, end up with a thousand dollars only. But then there is the deductive argument leading to the contrary conclusion that he is better off taking both boxes. Hence a contradiction, and we arrive at the conclusion that a reliable predictor with respect to a human player does not exist.

II

Finally we raise the question, what about a δ-machine which is programmed to randomize its choice through a strictly indeterministic physical process? The immediate answer seems to be that if the player is a δ-machine then its choices are unpredictable but that this does not affect our thesis concerning the unique freedom enjoyed by human beings. There remains, after all, a very significant difference between a human being and a mindless machine. In the case of the former we found that it was not necessary to postulate explicitly that it makes unpredictable choices; this conclusion imposed itself upon us and it follows from the fact that a human being is capable of having such mental properties as being desirous to achieve a certain aim and as being aware of a given argument as to how to secure this aim and then deciding to act in a way not conducive to achieving this aim.

But we can go further than this. Let our predictor be a person to whom physical indeterminacy is no obstacle, for he is capable of directly perceiving future events. In the case of a human player we know that even such a person cannot reliably predict what the choice is going to be because of the argument we have already repeated so many times in this part of our own book. But there is no reason why he should not be able to predict the choices of any machine, including a δ-machine. In maintaining this we are not led to any contradiction. For suppose the randomizer causes δ to choose box II only. The predictor looking into the future foresees this and puts $M in the box. What is the answer to the question 'Would δ have been better off by taking both boxes?' The answer from the perfect judge is, yes. There is no contrary answer based on past evidence. There is no support for saying that had it taken both boxes then it would have found the second box empty, for no machine with the same outcome of the random process has taken both boxes and ended up with a thousand dollars only, simply because no machine with the same outcome of the random process has taken both boxes.

Thus, all the relevant types of machines α, β, γ and δ are deprived of the kind of freedom enjoyed by a human being. Until somebody comes along and offers a description of a machine for which he can show that its choices are necessarily immune to any sort of prediction, I believe we are entitled to maintain that we have indeed succeeded in discovering a fundamental difference between people and mindless machines. A system which possesses a mind is unique in that in the case where he makes a decision which is free in the sense that it is not made contrary to his will, then his choice is unpredictable.

For a moment it might seem that one could ask the following question: what about a γ/δ machine, i.e., a machine which part of the time makes the choice that maximizes its gain and part of the time makes random choices? After all, when such a machine is in a γ-state and chooses both boxes we can ask what would have happened if it took box II only (since it is not the case that no machine of its kind ever chooses to take box II only) and hence expect an answer. But, of course, we must realize that it would have to be in a different state to take box II only, i.e., in a δ-state and with the randomizer determining that its choice is box II only, in which case, however, the predictor would have put money in box II. Thus had the machine been in a state in which it was determined to take box II only, it would have ended up with $M but even in that case it would have been better off if it took both boxes and gained $M plus $1000, except, of course, that it cannot do so not being in a δ-state and its choice being determined by the randomizer. Thus, by saying that all the choices of a γ/δ machine are predictable, we are not driven to give contradictory answers to any questions.

Once more we seem to be in the happy position of finding that a conclusion we arrived at through a fairly complex argument, may also be reached through entirely different routes. First of all I should like to remind the reader of the explanation offered for the past success of the predictor in the case of a human agent: P_i is not directly connected to C_i but to T_i and the predictor is, in fact, a perfect diagnostician of tendencies. However, the predictor will fail if the agent, through an exertion of his will, acts contrary to the tendency he has. It is quite clear, however, that it makes no sense to speak of a mindless machine, which by definition has no will, as exerting its will to act contrary to the tendency it has. Therefore the explanation why the predictor fails in the case of a human agent does not succeed when he is replaced by a machine.

Secondly, if we adopt the view that when two events, E_1 and

E_2 are causally connected, then if E_1 is a freely willed act which may possibly be accompanied by an intention to bring about E_2, then E_1 is the cause and E_2 the effect, then one more reason is provided why machine choices, unlike human choices, are in principle always predictable. In the case of a human agent this view entails that if C_i and P_i are causally connected then C_i is the cause of P_i and thus we would be confronted with an instance of backward causation. But in Chapter 15 we have offered a reason why backward causation may, in principle, be impossible. But no choice of a mindless machine can ever be described as 'free willed' or as 'performed with an intention'. Consequently there is no reason why, in the case of a machine, C_i and P_i should not be causally connected, since C_i need not be looked upon as the cause of P_i. Therefore there is no reason why all acts of all machines should not in principle, be predictable.

PART III

THE CONFIRMATION OF THEISM

CHAPTER 18

PASCAL'S WAGER

This part of the book is mainly devoted to discussing the positive arguments we may develop in favor of Theism by making use of what we have learnt from our study of modern science. Perhaps the best known instance in which a result of modern science was employed to support Theism, is Pascal's argument for Theism in which he makes use of what, nowadays, is called decision theory, a theory which he himself invented. I shall begin this part of our book by briefly reviewing Pascal's fairly well-known argument as it will lead to the appreciation of a number of instructive points. Pascal devised his argument not to show that Theism is true but rather that, irrespective of whether it is true or not, a rational person should treat it as true, and most important, he should try to behave in every way as if he knew it to be true.

Very briefly, the argument is based on the mathematical theory of expectations according to which, if one has the choice of betting on A or B and the probability that A wins is p and that B wins is q while the prizes A and B carry with them are a and b respectively, then the expectations associated with betting on A and B are ap and bq respectively. Thus the value one is receiving on being allowed to bet on A is ap and on B is bq. Now if it costs x to bet on A and y to bet on B, then as long as $ap - x > bq - y$ it is rational to bet on A.

A particular illustration is a horse race in which two horses, A and B, are running. Let the probability of A winning be ¾ while that of B winning be ¼ and also let us suppose that it costs nothing to bet on A while it costs \$5 to bet on B. However, A carries a prize of \$10 while B carries a prize of \$100. Here, ap = ¾ × \$10 = \$7.5, while bq = ¼ × \$100 = \$25 and $ap - x$ =

$7.5, while $bq - y$ = \$25 $-$ \$5 = \$20 and, thus in general, one should bet on B in spite of the fact that B is less likely to win and it costs money to bet on it, while it costs nothing to bet on A.

Now let A stand for agnosticism or atheism while B stands for a belief in God. We may not know exactly what numbers to assign to p and q in this case, however, we assume that they are both finite numbers. In life one has the option of betting on A or on B. To bet on A costs nothing, while one has to pay a certain amount for betting on B, because if a person wants to lead a life based on theism, he has to observe certain restrictions and cannot live a life of complete hedonism. However, if one bets on A and A wins, one wins nothing in the end, for there is nothing to follow this earthly life, while if one bets on B and B wins then one wins eternal salvation, which is the reward of all God-fearing people. Thus, even if the probability of A being true is larger than that of B being true, the expectation associated with A is zero, while that associated with B is infinite. Thus, even though there is a charge on betting on B, the charge is entirely negligible and hence it is rational to bet on B.[1]

The most immediate objection which springs to mind is that, unlike in the case of a horse race, when it comes to choosing a way of life, betting on B without actually believing in the truth of B may not secure for the winner the prize associated with B. It may well be questioned whether someone, who does not believe in God but leads a religious life only because prudence requires it as shown by Pascal, is to be deemed by Divine justice as entitled to salvation. Pascal assumes, however, that leading a religious life, no matter for what discreditable motives to begin with, inevitably leads to a genuine religious belief and devotion, since continual study and practice of religion and the association with pious

---

[1] A good recent discussion of Pascal's argument is to be found in I. Hacking, 'The Logic of Pascal's Wager', *American Philosophical Quarterly* (1972), pp. 186–92.

people is bound to convert the practitioner into a true believer in the teachings of theism. Hence it is advisable to embark upon a religious way of life out of prudence, since this will sooner or later transform a person into a genuinely convinced theist who will truly merit the reward of the pious.

There is, however, a more serious objection to Pascal. He seems to have made the entirely unrealistic assumption that by choosing a way of life one is faced with two options alone when, of course, there are indefinitely many. First of all it may be noted that a belief in God itself splits up into many distinct beliefs, namely a belief in God as conceived and prescribed by the various mono-theistic religions. Each of these religions promise eternal reward to those who pursue them and Pascal provides no argument to help one in selecting the right belief among these. Or consider D, which states that there is a very powerful demon who rules this universe and who rewards all those and only those who deny the existence of an omnipotent and omnibenevolent God, by granting them eternal bliss in the world to come. The expectation associated with D − no matter how minute the probability that D might be true − is infinitely large. Why choose B rather than D?

Some philosophers have, as a result of this objection, come to the conclusion that Pascal's argument has been shown to be entirely useless. Such a view may be warranted as long as one assumes that, in a situation in which betting on B and betting on D both carry infinite expectations, there can be no reason to prefer one to the other. There is, however, a different approach, which by no means seems unreasonable. According to it, when B and D equal one another as far as the expectations associated with them are concerned − both expectations being infinite − then we should choose the one which is more probable. On this latter view Pascal's wager is very useful to a large number of people.

Many people find themselves in the following situation: they find Naturalism very attractive and as a strong alternative candi-date to a belief in the existence of any supernatural power. If

Naturalism could be eliminated from being a viable choice for them and they were confined to make their selection from among hypotheses, all of which postulate some supernatural power, then one particular hypothesis would appear more credible to them than all others. A typical example is provided by someone who has been born to devout Roman Catholic parents and has never been troubled much by doubts that perhaps some other branch of Christianity represents the correct way to religion, and even less has he ever been worried that some other monotheistic religion might truly express God's will to be worshipped. Other ideologies postulating supernatural powers have hardly ever even entered his mind. However, due to the secular education he has received since early adolescence, his training as a scientist and his constant association with agnostics, he has become exposed to the attractions of a naturalistic world-view and thus he often finds that his grip upon his faith is loosening and he is wondering whether the truth might not be that reality consists of nothing more than the entities, forces and processes acknowledged by modern science.

To such a person Pascal provides all the help he needs and the problem, with respect to which Pascal has no assistance to offer, does not arise anyhow. According to his argument, someone who is about to choose a way of life has to divide all the possible beliefs about the universe, its origin, purpose and the purpose of man's life, if any, into two classes. Class A of beliefs contains all those ideologies which do not promise, to those who embrace them, eternal bliss while every member of class B does. Pascal's argument leads to the conclusion that a rational person must adopt a belief which belongs to class B. Admittedly his argument does not help one at all to select a particular belief among all those which belong to B, but it does eliminate the problem the typical person has. For now he is left to choose his belief from the class of beliefs where he is pretty confident which one he should regard as the most likely to be true.

We should, therefore, acknowledge the great significance of

Pascal's argument. It may, of course, be of interest ot inquire what precisely are the reasons why the great majority of people would resolutely reject a hypothesis like D in favour of Theism. It is, however, not necessary that we do so in order to see the power of Pascal's argument in providing support for Theism against what most people regard as a viable rival.

It seems to me, from my reading Penelhum's *Religion and Rationality* (N.Y., 1971), that he would be willing to agree to practically everything I have said so far concerning Pascal's argument, yet in the end he concludes that the argument fails. On page 218, he says:

If it is true that men can hear and not be convinced, then unbelief does not necessarily equal self-deception. But then unbelief does not necessarily merit exclusion from salvation. If it does not, then Pascal's Wager argument, which presupposes that it does, is morally unworthy of acceptance. Perhaps, of course, it is not a necessary feature of Christian doctrine to insist that unbelief entails exclusion from salvation. But in that case again, Pascal's Wager ceases to have any point.

I do not find this argument particularly damaging. People can hear a great deal of compelling evidence concerning the harmfulness of tobacco or alcohol yet, because of a weakness of will, yield to their cravings for these and thus allow themselves to become victims of self-deception. It is not, therefore, implausible for Pascal to hold that there are compelling arguments why one should adhere to a theistic way of life (e.g., Pascal's argument), yet many will nevertheless succumb to the attraction an irreligious way of life holds out for them. They may, therefore, deserve exclusion from salvation.

There are, however, two points which I must now make. Firstly, even to a person who considers Naturalism as the only plausible rival to the particular brand of Theism he would otherwise readily embrace, Pascal's argument on its own does not do everything there is to be accomplished. After all, to know that it is most rational to adopt the way prescribed by Theism is not to know all there is to know; we may also be interested in the truth as such and want to know whether Theism is more likely to be true than its denial. An enlightened person, even when he knows that he has to cultivate a belief in Theism, may still quest for the sake of intellectual satisfaction to know if there is any good evidence in support of it.

Secondly, it should be realized that there are ways in which Pascal's argument could be rendered entirely ineffective. One way would be to prove conclusively that God does not exist, in consequence of which the probability of Theism would become zero and then, of course, it is no longer true that the expectations associated with a theistic way of life are infinite (since, if $a = \infty$ and $p = o$, then ap is of an indeterminate value). This, however, is a rather unlikely way. But there is also the possibility of showing that the sentence 'God exists' is meaningless, hence it has no truth value at all, in which case the probability that Theism is true is once more zero and Pascal's argument collapses. There have been quite a number of philosophers who have held the view that Theism is indeed devoid of all meaning. It is to the discussion of this view that we shall now turn our attention.

CHAPTER 19

THEISM AND THE VERIFICATION PRINCIPLE

Recently, people with a strong empiricist bent, which may be said to be an outlook strongly inspired by modern science, have intensified their attacks on Theism. Instead of just claiming that Theism is not well founded and, therefore there are no reasons to believe it true, they have raised a more fundamental objection, denying that it has any meaning at all. According to this line of attack on Theism, not only is there nothing in our experience which confirms it, but in principle it is impossible that we could ever find experience confirming, or for that matter disconfirming, a belief in God. Any conceivable state of affairs is compatible both with the truth and the falsity of Theism; it makes no difference to what we might ever observe whether God exists or not. It is wrong, therefore, to assume that the theistic claim is a factual claim and that it has any cognitive significance. Hence, the question whether one should believe in the existence of God does not even arise. Sensible people do not altogether concern themselves with religious utterances which amount to empty verbiage. Even with the most pious intentions one cannot believe that the sentence 'God exists' expresses a true proposition when that sentence expresses no proposition at all, being altogether devoid of meaning.

This new line of attack, according to which Theism is not false but worse, meaningless, because unverifiable and unfalsifiable has been employed by a number of philosophers, but has become widely known through the arguments of A. Flew.[1] It is fair to state that his challenge has constituted a major milestone in recent

---

[1] *New Essays in Philosophical Theology*, ed. A. Flew and A. MacIntyre (London, 1955), p. 96.

theistic controversy. Its effects have been quite devastating. More efforts have been made to try and repair the damage done by him to the cause of theism in recent years than to meet any other challenge.

There were some who thought that it would be wiser not to directly oppose Flew's irresistible thrust but to radically revise Theism so that it becomes immune to it. R. M. Hare, for example, concedes

...on the ground marked out by Flew he seems to me to be completely victorious.[2]

He then goes on to claim that religious utterances are not to be construed as assertions about how the world is, their function, instead, is to express the kind of basic attitude the believer has to life, for which he introduced the term 'blik'. Hare's approach reflects the idea that the new type of unbelief calls for a new type of belief. Contemporary atheism does not denounce religious affirmations as false, but as meaningless verbiage; the appropriate defense is not to insist upon the factual truth of theistic doctrines and admit that they are not congnitively meaningful, but plead that they are not therefore entirely useless.

Traditionally minded theists might be forgiven if they view Hare's ultra progressive position (which is also that of Braithwaite, expounded in considerable detail in his well known *An Empiricist's View of the Nature of Religious Belief*) as being somewhat to the left of a good old-fashioned atheist. The latter, though he declares Theism as definitely false, nevertheless concedes that it succeeds in expressing what it means. They may even feel less comfortable with Hare's tactics than with the maneuverings of the inimitable Rev. Mackarel, who is reported by Peter De Vries to have declared: 'It is the final proof of God's omnipotence that he need not exist in order to save us.'

---

[2] *Ibid.*, p. 99.

But of course, not everybody is yet ready to surrender classical Theism according to which a belief in God is a belief in the factuality of a most important aspect of the universe. The natural reaction to Flew is to attempt to claim that his criterion of what is meaningful does not apply everywhere; that it, of course, applies everywhere within scientific discourse, where it was first developed, but not in religious discourse. It is very difficult, however, to develop such a suggestion in detail without it leading to Hare's position, since the justification for maintaining such a difference lies ultimately in the assumption that, while scientific discourse is about the world and therefore must in some way be rooted in an observable aspect of the world, religious discourse is not. Not willing to embrace this position, some have gone to the extreme of denying that the verification principle applies anywhere. For example, Schubert M. Ogden says:

Even scientific utterances, it appears, are far from completely homogeneous and some of the more fundamental of them are as little able to survive a strict application of the 'verification principle' as any of the utterances of religion.[3]

Now it may be true that any one of the formal versions of the verification principle, put forward in an attempt to state exactly the conditions which are universally satisfied by all cognitively meaningful sentences, has turned out to be such that some sentences, which are generally approved as scientific sentences, violate them. But this only shows that no particular attempt to formally state a criterion of verifiability, has so far succeeded. It is justifiable, however, to insist that, in the case of any particular legitimate scientific sentence, we can easily show how it is rooted in experience. What seems much more difficult to do, is to be able to abstract a particular feature of the way in which a given sentence is ultimately linked to observation and point to it as being, in

---

[3] 'Falsification and Belief', *Religious Studies* (1974), p. 22.

general, the essential feature, which all sentences that are, in principle, verifiable, possess. In other words, we have not been able to articulate or discover what is basically common among all verifiable sentences. But we can judge in every individual case whether a given sentence is or is not verifiable in principle and it is quite clear, in spite of Ogden's claim that his conclusion is the 'generally accepted result of analysis', that there is not a single sentence which the scientific community accepts as true and is not manifestly confirmed by experience, nor a question which scientists regard as meaningful yet an answer to it is not believed, in principle, as possible of confirmation.

Another brave attempt to fight Flew without flinching from adopting what to me seem quite desperate measures, is made by J. Kellenberger. He says:

> It may not be the case that the believer who says that there is a God has tied to his statement a verification or falsification condition, but then most typically he is not offering a hypothesis. He is not tentatively explaining anything. He is affirming what he believes.
> . . .
> The relationship that a believer affirms is, or quite often is, one of trust. If one did impart the attitude appropriate to advancing a hypothesis to affirming a belief, a relationship would be subverted. One cannot affirm a relationship of trust by tentatively offering a judgement that is tied to a falsification condition.[4]

Kellenberger maintains that the verification principle is to be applied to all hypotheses, and to hypotheses only. A hypothesis is essentially something that is advanced tentatively and is held conditionally. To the theist the proposition 'God exists' is not a hypothesis at all since he advances it with certainty and his commitment to it is not subject to possible revision. The basis for maintaining or withdrawing a hypothesis is confirmatory or disconfirmatory evidence which may be forthcoming. A hypothesis

---

[4] J. Kellenberger, 'The Falsification Challenge', *Religious Studies* (1969), pp. 75—6.

may therefore not even be entertained as meaningful unless it can be shown that, in principle, evidence may be available whereby to judge its truth or falsity. The basis for maintaining a belief like a belief in God, is trust. The believer proclaims his faith without demanding any evidence for its truth, hence the meaningfulness of his belief is not to be judged by the criterion of the availability of evidence either.

But surely, even Kellenberger agrees that some sentences are nonsensical and with the greatest eagerness to believe, one cannot confer meaning upon that which is unintelligible. Thus, while faith and trust may be sufficient for the believer to regard the sentences he affirms as true, the question of whether that sentence is meaningful in the first place has to be settled prior to, and independently of, his willingness to believe in it. This question is to be always settled, according to Flew, by the application of the verification principle. Kellenberger has not suggested an alternative method which is to be used in judging the meaningfulness of sentences, which when they are held true, are held true without evidence and unconditionally.

Another attempt to avoid Flew's objection has already been alluded to in Part I and consists of the claim that theism, while unverifiable in this life, may be verifiable in the after-life through a more direct confrontation with the Divine. I can, however, imagine how an atheist might challenge the validity of this defense. The exact nature of this confrontation has not been specified. Thus, the question he will pose is this: are these unspecified experiences in the after-life describable or, because of their 'otherworldly' character, ineffable? If they are describable then he will ask why drag the after-life into this, since there can be no reason why it is logically impossible for coherently depictable experiences to take place in the here and now? Thus, presumably they are indescribable. If so, what evidence do we have that they are logically possible experiences?

Finally, I should like to discuss Plantinga's defense of theism against Flew's attack, who perhaps may be said to develop his ideas in greater detail than others. Plantinga's defense is similar to Ogden's in that he too claims that the verification principle is not binding. His argument, however, is not that the principle is violated in science, but that no attempt to clearly formulate it has so far been successful; and, hence, no one really knows what it is. It may well be that in any individual case of a sentence generally acknowledged as cognitively meaningful, we can explain in what way it is tied to experience, but as long as we cannot describe the notion of confirmability in principle, in accurate general terms we cannot be sure that we are dealing with a legitimate notion nor whether the principle requiring that all empirically significant sentences must be confirmable is, strictly speaking, meaningful.

Plantinga surveys the various attempts which were made, mainly in the thirties and forties of this century, to set up a criterion against which one could test any sentence, whether or not it was to be regarded as verifiable. Those who were engaged in setting up these various criteria supposed that a sentence S is verifiable if and only if S had such and such connection to some observation sentence O. It was recognized from the beginning, that it is certainly not required that S should have the strongest possible connection to observation, namely that S be entailed by O; furthermore, that it is not even required that S on its own entails O. It was thought that in order that S be confirmable it was sufficient if S entailed O conjointly with some other sentences. The problem then was to describe the form which the auxiliary sentences A must take, together with which S may entail O. It is obvious that A cannot be allowed to entail O on its own, since then S would be entirely redundant. But A must also be further restricted since, if any A be allowed, then it can be shown, as it has been shown, that no matter what S stands for we can always find some A together with which S will entail O, not entailed by A alone. If on the other hand, we place too many restrictions on the form A may take we find that many S's, which are regarded by scientists as highly significant, are ruled out as meaningless by our criterion. Various A's, which seemed neither too liberal nor too restrictive, were suggested but were subsequently shown inadequate upon which these suggestions were revised only to be found inadequate again. Eventually the chances began to look very dim that anybody would ever succeed in constructing a satisfactory criterion. This is how Plantinga sees the situation at present:

> The fact is that no one has succeeded in stating a version of the verifiability criterion that is even remotely plausible; and by now the project is beginning to look unhopeful.[5]

In order to strengthen his case Plantinga could have also mentioned that, seeing the repeated failure of philosophers to come up with a meaning criterion for sentences which was not too restrictive to rule out important scientific sentences and also not too permissive to let through what is obvious nonsense, Carnap proposed a change of strategy and suggested that instead of attempting to deal with whole sentences we set up a criterion to test the meaningfulness of single terms.[6] He proposed a five-point criterion against which every term is to be tested before it is admitted into meaningful discourse. The main trouble with Carnap's approach is that a term meaningful in one context may not be meaningful in another context and that ultimately, therefore, we are driven to testing the meaningfulness of sentences again — a hopeless enterprise by Carnap's own judgment.

In addition to stressing the improbability that we shall ever hit upon a satisfactory formulation of the verifiability principle, Plantinga — for added safety no doubt — also advances the suggestion that the principle may apply in science but not necessarily in theology. He does not develop this point in detail. It is a point which on the surface does not square very well with his general

[5] *God and Other Minds*, p. 167.
[6] 'The Methodological Character of Theoretical Concepts', *Minnesota Studies in the Philosophy of Science*, Vol. I (Minnesota, 1958), pp. 38–76.

position that theological statements are factual statements. Concerning his point about the consistent failure to construct an adequate criterion of verification he says:

In the light ... of the fact that it seems impossible to state the verifiability criterion the question becomes acute: how *are* we to understand Flew's challenge? What exactly is he requiring of theological statements? Is he chiding the theist for ignoring some version of the verifiability criterion? If so which version? Until these questions are answered it is impossible to determine whether his challenge is legitimate or even what the challenge *is*. If the notion of verifiability cannot so much as be explained, if we cannot so much as say what it is for a statement to be empirically verifiable, then we scarcely need worry about whether religious statements are or are not verifiable. How could we possibly tell? As a piece of natural atheology, verificationism is entirely unsuccessful.[7]

In a footnote he expresses puzzlement over theologians who felt constrained to revise their doctrines in the light of the verification principle. If only they had studied the principle more carefully they would have realized that there was no need to rush to embrace it.

The plausibility of Plantinga's argument further increases once we note that the same assessment of the status of the verification principle has been made by many others, who arrived at their conclusion without being driven to it by a particular desire to defend Theism against the charge of meaninglessness. Not so long ago, for example, three philosophers, in a paper which makes no reference to religion, summarize the situation in which the verification may be said to be these days, in this way:

Increasingly subtle attempts to specify the relation that must obtain between a sentence if the sentence is to be verifiable fell upon increasingly subtle counterexamples. Gradually the program's supporters have lost faith.[8]

[7] *God and Other Minds*, p. 168.
[8] Stephen P. Stich, John Tinnon and Lawrence Sklar 'Entailment and the Verification Program', *Ratio* (1973), p. 84.

CHAPTER 20

THE VINDICATION OF THE VERIFICATION PRINCIPLE

For reasons I shall endeavor to make clear in this chapter, I do not go along with the opinion that the verification principle is altogether to be abandoned. I admit that for many years I have been struggling with the puzzle of verificationism. On the one hand it always seemed to me that some very liberal version, which only demands that there be a minimal connection between a cognitively meaningful non-analytic sentence and experience, must be correct. After all, a sentence which has absolutely no observational footings, even in the remotest sense of that term, cannot be expressing a statement about the world. As Herbert Feigl is fond of saying, 'a difference must make a difference', and if any state of the world is compatible with a given sentence then how can it make any difference whether we affirm or deny that sentence; and if indeed we say that it makes no difference then that amounts to saying that the sentence is devoid of meaning. On the other hand, so many attempts to set up a verification criterion have failed that even many former adherents of verificationism are now prepared to entertain second thoughts about the matter.

There are two points, however, which have made me reluctant to concede the unviability of verificationism and hope that eventually we shall discover a common erroneous assumption which is responsible for the failure of all the attempts to set up a suitable criterion.

One point I have already made before: we do not seem to have any difficulty in distinguishing between unverifiable sentences and verifiable ones. When confronted with a sentence which is generally deemed meaningful, we can explain why it is regarded as verifiable. In other words, we know verifiability when we see it, it is just that we have not succeeded in picking out the common feature in the relationship all verifiable sentences have to observation.

Another, more important point is this. While people may object to the enunciation of the principle that a sentence is meaningful if and only if it is confirmable, no one objects to proclaiming the rule that a proposition is credible only if it is confirmed. Everyone agrees that no proposition ought to be accepted as likely to be true unless there is evidence supporting it more than any of its contraries, that is, unless it is confirmed more than any of its contraries. It is also agreed that whenever evidence supports a proposition considerably more than any of its contraries, that is, whenever a proposition is confirmed to a high degree, we regard it as credible. Thus, while more and more philosophers urge us to give up the idea of tying meaningfulness to confirmability in principle, nobody has ever suggested that we ought to give up our habit of tying credibility to being actually confirmed. It has not been claimed that the term 'being confirmed' is a vague term of which we do not know exactly what it stands for. It is assumed that in any specified state of knowledge, be it actual or possible, we can determine whether or not a proposition is confirmed. And even if there are some exceptional situations in which we would be at a loss to say whether a given proposition should or should not be regarded as confirmed, this would not render the concept of confirmation useless. We would still insist that credibility is always tied to confirmation except that in some cases, it may not be clear whether or not a proposition was confirmed by a given observation and hence we would not know in those particular cases whether the proposition in question should be regarded as having increased its credibility relative to what it was in the absence of that observation. But if there is no problem with the term 'confirmed' there should be no problem with the term 'confirmable' either. After all, we can define 'confirmable' in terms of 'confirmed': a sentence is confirmable if, and only if, circumstances can coherently be described under which it would be confirmed.

But suppose it is asked, how do matters stand with respect to a clearly stated criterion whereby all sentences can be tested whether or not they are confirmed by the available evidence? First of all let me say that as far as our inquiries are concerned it does not matter at all what the answer to this question is. To whatever degree the concept of confirmation is clear, to that degree, the concept of confirmability in principle is clear also by virtue of the complete definability of the latter in terms of the former. And if our understanding of the notion of confirmation is seriously deficient, because all attempts to set up such a criterion have failed, then so is our understanding of the notion of confirmability. But this in no way provides a justification for wanting to divorce meaningfulness from confirmability, just as no one wishes to separate credibility from confirmation. It so happens that a good deal of work has been done on the concept of confirmation and there are a number of results all more or less agreed upon, but there are also some unsolved problems left. There exist, for instance, what are known as the paradoxes of confirmation, but these, rather than be taken as signs that the whole idea of confirmation is incoherent and should be discarded, are looked upon as a source of challenge to do more clarificatory work. It seems that since the belief in the intimate connection between confirmation and credibility is an old and established one, those who have been working on the philosophy of confirmation did not feel the need to justify themselves; there has been no rush to try to capture in one fell swoop the notion of confirmation and set up in a couple of brief sentences a criterion of confirmation. In fact, philosophers rather than trying to enunciate a criterion of confirmation, prefer to talk about a whole theory of confirmation which is to be constructed. This implies that there are a number of conditions with all sorts of qualifications, which can only, over a long period, be gradually put together. Philosophers were much more hurried when it came to the notion of confirmability. Apparently, because of the need to gain converts to the novel idea of defining cognitive meaningfulness in terms of confirmability in principle, they tried a short cut, and instead of defining confirmability in terms of confirmation as they should have, they attempted to quickly construct a neat criterion whereby results would be mass-produced in a mechanical fashion.

I find it quite fascinating that the reason why the numerous efforts to produce a concise definition of the notion of verifiability have failed, turns out to be, indeed, an important erroneous presupposition common to all these efforts. This emerges very clearly, for instance, upon considering I. Scheffler's very useful work which has dealt at great length with the issue before us. Scheffler explains that while philosophers may not know how to properly define the criterion of verifiability they are after, they have a clear notion what general conditions such a criterion would have to satisfy. In other words, we have a number of criteria of adequacy for an acceptable verifiability criterion. According to Scheffler, the first criterion of adequacy is:

For every sentence S, S is true or false if, and only if, S is significant.[1]

This criterion of adequacy (in which he uses the somewhat more restricted term 'significant' rather than 'meaningful') is most certainly one everybody would wish to adopt. As he explains, it allows us to rule out as inadequate any suggested criterion whereby some sentences satisfying the criterion were neither true nor false, or if it ruled out any sentence as devoid of significance even though that sentence was true or false. His third criterion of adequacy for instance runs as follows:

It is not the case that for every sentence S, S is significant.

Once more a very reasonable requirement. In fact this criterion of adequacy has very often been employed to expose the inadequacy of various suggested criteria of verifiability — they were shown to

[1] *The Anatomy of Inquiry* (New York, 1963), p. 129.

be too permissive and their adoption would have led to the admission of every sentence as significant, in which case, of course, we do not need any criterion in the first place to test the empirical significance of sentences. But the really interesting criterion of adequacy is his second which goes as follows:

There is some logical relation R, such that for every sentence S, S is significant if, and only if, S is analytic or related by R to some observation sentence O.[2]

This criterion is profoundly wrong. Scheffler is certainly right however in claiming that everyone has assumed it to be a correct criterion. The presupposition that Scheffler's second criterion of adequacy is a correct criterion is then the erroneous presupposition common to all the efforts to set up a verifiability-criterion, a presupposition which fully explains the failure of these efforts.

There is simply no relationship whatever between a sentence S and an observation sentence O which on its own can secure the confirmability of S. S is never confirmed by an established O by virtue of it being related in some way to O alone, unless it is the case that S is entailed by O and then, of course, S itself is an observation sentence. But suppose S has the required relation R to an established observation sentence O, which under normal circumstances ensures that the credibility of S rises through O. If it should turn out to be the case that ∼ S has precisely the same relation R to the same O, then surely it stands to reason that the credibility of S could not really have risen through the presence of O since that of ∼ S would have risen just as much. Thus it must be the correct thing to say that even though R is the crucial relationship which a given sentence needs, in general, to have to an established observation sentence in order to receive confirmation, when both S and the denial of S have R to an established O, then neither of them receives any confirmation. Thus Scheffler's second

---

[2]   *Ibid.*, p. 132.

criterion of adequacy would come much nearer to the truth if it ran as follows:

There is some logical relation R, such that for every sentence S, S is significant, if, an only if, S is analytic or related by R to some observation sentence O, and it is not the case that ~ S is also related by R to the same observation sentence O.

It will be instructive to consider a criterion of verification which was suggested at an early stage in the history of verificationism and which was constructed on the basis of the acceptance of Scheffler's original criteria of adequacy. A. J. Ayer suggested the criterion according to which S is empirically significant if, and only if, in conjunction with additional premises, S logically implies some observation statement O not implied by these additional premises alone. This suggestion has been found faulty, indeed as violating the third criterion of adequacy, by I. Berlin. Berlin has shown that no matter what S stands for it would pass as verifiable by Ayer's principle. Let S stand for any sentence: then by *modus ponens*, S & (S ⊃ O) logically imply O which is not implied by the additional premise S ⊃ O alone.[3]

Imagine however, if Ayer had been somewhat more circumspective, taking into account what we have just said. He would then have qualified his criterion expressing it in this way:

S is empirically significant if and only if in conjunction with additional premises, S logically implies some observation statement not implied by these additional premises alone and it is not the case that also S in conjunction with additional premises logically implies the same observation statements not implied by these additional premises alone.

It can be seen at once that Berlin's criticism would have become entirely ineffective. True enough no matter what S stands for, S & (S ⊃ O) logically implies O. But then it is also true that ~ S &

---

[3] 'Verifiability in Principle', *Proceedings of the Aristotelian Society* (1939), pp. 225–8.

($\sim$ S $\supset$ O) logically implies O. Consequently the confirmability of neither S, nor of $\sim$ S has been established.

What a simple qualification is being suggested here: yet what a big difference it would have made to an important section in the history of analytic philosophy. Ayer would have never been forced to abandon his original criterion and replace it by a more complex one. As it happens this more complex criterion was overturned by Church moving Nidditch to suggest a modified criteria which, however, was shown inadequate by Scheffler. The reader can see for himself, by reading Scheffler's account of these attacks,[4] that Church's attack as well as Scheffler's attack would like Berlin's attack, have come to nil if the simple qualification suggested here had been incorporated into Ayer's criterion.

Some people may still wish to object, that though far less frequently mentioned, there is another reason why verificationism had to be abandoned. They will point out that no one has been successful in giving a clear definition of what should count as an observation statement in contradistinction to a theoretical statement. After all, the central claim of·verificationism is that every meaningful S has R to an observation statement. But as we do not know what an observation statement is, verificationism collapses.

Once more the reply to this is that we do not give up the concept of confirmation just because of this difficulty, for even if we do not know what precisely an observation statement is, we regard a hypothesis as confirmed if it bears a certain relation to a statement we all agree, for whatever reason, is true. Similarly we regard a sentence as meaningful if it has R to a sentence which under given circumstances all would agree, expressed a true statement, while the denial of that sentence does not have that R to the same statement. But then this presupposes that there are certain privileged sentences whose meaningfulness is not in question? Definitely so. It is not necessary to take verificationism to be the attitude which

---

[4]   *Anatomy of Inquiry*, pp. 150–4.

refuses to treat any sentence as meaningful until it is proven so by the application of the verification criterion. It is not unreasonable to hold that the question of meaningfulness is not raised with respect to any sentence that is generally regarded as true or false, whether we can or cannot give a precise account why it is generally so regarded. It is only with respect to a sentence S, whose truth value is unknown, that we raise the doubt, perhaps S is not even meaningful and will not be reassured on this matter until shown that S has R to a sentence which we know, that under certain circumstances all would agree, was true or false. Thus O should no longer denote an 'observation statement' but the kind of statement just described.

Let me also mention that I would further modify Ayer's qualified criterion by not insisting that S logically implies O and be satisfied also merely if the probability of O is higher on S than on ~ S. Also we should concede the meaningfulness of S if it is logically implied by a confirmable sentence.

Thus we can answer in full all of Plantinga's questions. He asks how *are* we to understand Flew's challenge? What exactly is he requiring of theological statements? Is he chiding the theist for ignoring some version of the verifiability criterion? If so, which version? The answers are: Flew requires — and it does not seem unreasonable to require — that statements which purport to be statements describing how the world is conform to the verifiability principle to which all statements, the meaningfulness of which is to be established, conform. The version of the principle to which theological statements and all other such statements have to comply is, of course, the correct version which may be simply worded 'A sentence is confirmable if, and only if, circumstances are describable under which it would be regarded as confirmed on the basis of prevailing tenets of scientific methodology'. One may, if one wishes, give a more elaborate version and offer Ayer's criterion the way it has been qualified here, substituting 'confirmable' for 'empirically significant'.

CHAPTER 21

THE PRINCIPLES UNDERLYING
SCIENTIFIC METHOD

I

But the way to answer Flew's challenge is to show that Theism is confirmable in principle. In fact it is confirmed in practice. In Part II I have already indicated the kind of evidence which may be regarded as confirming Theism, however, that was done without first providing a basic clarification of elementary confirmation theory, which I propose to do here. I need not enter into any of the more elaborate aspects of scientific methodology. I am not going to say anything about degrees of confirmation nor much about the question in what circumstances a hypothesis is to be accepted as true. All I wish to discuss is the general circumstances under which a given piece of evidence E may be said to raise the credibility of hypothesis H relative to its contradictory or contrary to a level higher than it would have been in the absence of E. I shall be dealing with two elementary principles to be called Principle A and Principle E. I shall begin with the latter:

> *Principle E*: when a given piece of evidence E is more probable on H than on H' then E confirms H more than H'.

This I believe should appear very reasonable to everyone and can be shown to be so in various ways. After all, when the probability of E on H is zero, that is when $p(E/H) = 0$, then E falsifies H, thus the further $p(E/H)$ is from zero the less E falsifies H or the more it confirms it. Or, one may say, the hypothesis we wish to adopt is to account for E, and it is clear, a hypothesis on which E is highly improbable does not account for E; in fact the very meaning of the expression 'account for' implies that the more an hypothesis makes E probable the more it may be said to account for it.

We may look at some examples illustrating Principle E at work.

Let h_1 = All ravens are black.
       h_2 = Ravens come in more than one color.
       e_1 = Of the five ravens hitherto observed all were black.

Here we have a paradigm example of evidence supporting a hypothesis; the credibility of h_1 as compared to h_2 rises through e, and obviously

$$p(e_1/h_1) > p(e_1/h_2)$$

It may be noted that although e_1 confirms h_1 relative to h_2 it does not necessarily mean that we will subscribe to h_1 rather than to h_2 now that e_1 is given, since the initial credibility of h_2 may have been considerably higher than that of h_1 in view of the fact that members of other species of birds in general come in a variety of colors.

Another example we may look at concerns a hypothesis which is not a universal generalization. Suppose a friend of ours claims that he is a perfect healer of all diseases and that by simply laying his hands upon the head of any sick person, if he so wishes, he is capable of curing that person from whatever is ailing him. We will denote by k_1 the hypothesis advanced by our friend; and see how it fares in comparison with k_2, which is held by everyone else, that our friend is nothing of the kind, but is an ordinary person without any startling abilities. Suppose we observe that e_2, i.e., that our friend, when confronted by someone who has been suffering from ulcers for years, lays his hands upon that person's head and he promptly recovers from his illness. Everyone will agree that e_2 increases the credibility of k_1 relative to k_2. But here once more

$$p(e_2/k_1) > p(e_2/k_2)$$

which explains why e_2 confirms k_1, relative to k_2. Again of course, it does not follow that upon obtaining e_2 we shall accept k_1 as true, since, given our background knowledge concerning miracle healers, k_1 has much less credibility to begin with than k_2; and e_2 may not raise the credibility of k_1 sufficiently to render it preferable to k_2.

We may now look once more at the claim made in Part II that the observed nature of human beings may be construed as evidence confirming Theism. Let

> C = Humans are always constrained to act contrary to their wills.

If we lived in a world in which C was true − and surely such a world seems logically possible − then human beings could not be said to be free, in any sense of the word. Many theists agree that $T \rightarrow \sim C$, i.e., that Theism logically implies that C is false. On the other hand, of course, both C and $\sim C$ are compatible with N (Naturalism). Consequently

$$p(\sim C/T) > p(\sim C/N)$$

from which it follows that the fact that $\sim C$ is true confirms T relative to N. Of course there are Theists who demand that not only $\sim C$ be true but something seemingly stronger, namely that

> F = There are some human acts which are in principle unpredictable,

be also true. However, as we have shown in Part II, $\sim C$ logically implies F, because in a situation in which a person can do exactly what he wishes, some of his acts can, in principle, not be predicted, as is demonstrated through the contradiction deriveable from Game 1 when matters are assumed to be otherwise.

II

What I have said concerning Principle E is quite commonly assumed to be true. A principle very similar to it has even explicitly been formulated by J. L. Mackie.[1] The only substantial difference between his principle and mine is that instead of saying 'When a given piece of evidence etc' he says 'If and only if'. This, I have to emphasize, is an important mistake. H is more confirmed than H' by E *if* $p(E/H) > p(E/H')$ but not *only* if. The reason is that it is often the case that H and H' are related exactly in the same way to all the available evidence, yet we regard H as more confirmed than H' simply because we find H intrinsically more adequate. This brings us to Principle A which is a principle of adequacy. It is best introduced by illustrating it with what may be called Jeffreys' problem.

Suppose we have a very large number of observations concerning the distances covered by freely falling objects near the surface of the earth and the duration of the fall, and they all fit hypothesis G — first advanced by Galileo — that the law governing the correlation between distance and time is given by

$$s = \tfrac{1}{2} g t^2$$

where 's' stands for 'distance', 't' for time and 'g' is constant. Then it immediately follows that all the observations are in complete accordance with the contrary hypothesis J_1, claiming that the equation representing the correlation in question is given by

$$s = \tfrac{1}{2} g t^2 + f_1(x)$$

where $f_1(x)$ is a peculiar kind of function of some variable x equalling zero for all the observations hitherto made, but not necessarily for any future observations.[2] In the same way there are also the rival hypotheses J_2, J_3 etc., which have, instead of $f_1(x)$,

---

[1] He calls it, Principle C_2, cf. his 'The Relevance Criterion of Confirmation', *British J. Phil. Science* (1969), pp. 27–40.
[2] For a more detailed discussion of this see Chapter 2 of my *Confirmation and Confirmability*.

the extra expressions $f_2(x)$, $f_3(x)$ etc. that have the same peculiarity as $f_1(x)$. Why is it then that even though

$$p(O/G) = p(O/J_1) = p(O/J_2) = p(O/J_3) = \cdots = 1$$

where O stands for the observed correlation of time and distance, we nevertheless regard G as much more confirmed by O than by any one of the J-hypotheses? The answer that Jeffreys gives, and which is no doubt the right answer, is that G is the simplest hypothesis postulating the most parsimonious equation. While in general, simplicity is a very problematic notion, in this case matters are very straightforward. All the equations postulated by the J-hypotheses have the terms of the equation postulated by G, but also at least one extra term of varying complexity. So obviously the equations associated with the J-hypotheses are less parsimonious. G then is regarded as intrinsically more adequate than any one of the J-hypothesis because of its maximum simplicity. We may thus formulate our principle of adequacy as:

> *Principle A*: When H and H′ are similarly related to all the available evidence, we regard H as more confirmed than H′, if and only, H is more adequate than H′.

This, of course, leaves us with the vital question, what features of a hypothesis contribute to its adequacy? In particular, why should the greater simplicity of G render it more adequate in the sense that it has to be treated as more confirmed than all its rivals?

III

In order to provide an answer to the questions just raised let us for a moment consider how I would behave if I took Jeffreys' problem as unsolved and worried greatly therefore, whether G, J_1 or any other one of the infinitely many hypotheses accounting equally well for all past observations is most likely to be true. It is clear that Jeffreys' problem affects equally every hypothesis normally entertained by us since each one has infinitely many rivals which logically imply all the available evidence. It would seem then that I would not, for one further moment, remain inside this building since according to some of the hypotheses concerning the future state of the roof, it is just about to collapse. But I cannot stand on the ground outside the building either for it will melt beneath my feet according to some of the rivals to the generally held hypothesis postulating the continuing solidity of the ground. But then I cannot go anywhere nor stay here, which is, of course, impossible without being destroyed. I would also have to stop breathing, since the hypothesis that the air will turn into poison gas the next moment is just as well confirmed as the one postulating that it will not; but then I must not stop breathing for there are well confirmed hypotheses according to which breathing is essential to life. This is quite enough to show clearly that it is really impossible for me to act in keeping with my skepticism, for that would entail my refraining from doing A as well as my refraining from not doing A at the same time. I cannot exercise the caution that my skepticism would require me to exercise and refrain from adopting any line of action. Thus, even if I did not believe at all in the efficacy of Principle A to lead to credible hypotheses, I still may wish to adopt a set of hypotheses which imply that in every situation a given line of action rather than its opposite is to be adopted.

Suppose then that all I wanted from my hypotheses is a clear instruction as to how to act. Would I then be satisified with just any guiding rule for hypothesis selection? It is obvious that a rule which did not guide me to the selection of a specific hypothesis to confer confirmation on it would be quite useless. For example, when faced with G and all the J-hypotheses, if I were given the guiding rule, 'select the hypothesis with the least parsimonious equation', this would lead me nowhere. No matter how complex an equation, a more complex one can always be constructed. But suppose I was given the rule 'select the hypothesis postulating the second most parsimonious equation'. It can easily be seen that this would still not lead me to a specific hypothesis. For let us assume that all are willing to agree that of all the f's, f_n is the simplest. It follows then that

$$s = \frac{1}{2} g t^2 + f_n(x)$$

is the second most parsimonious equation. But x may stand for indefinitely many different physical parameters and our rule says nothing about what one should denote x in the hypothesis to be selected. Thus, only the rule 'select the hypothesis postulating the most parsimonious equation' leads us to a specific hypothesis namely to G!

This enables us at once to define clearly the term 'adequate' which appears in Principle A: the most adequate hypothesis is the one selected with the aid of the only useable guiding rule.

For a moment it might appear that we have gone too far too soon. Surely, some may wish to object, there must be other rules with will lead to the selection of a specific hypothesis among all the available hypotheses. What about the rule 'select the hypothesis designated by the Vice President of the U.S.'. Should the V.P. agree to spend his spare time in picking out one hypothesis from each one of the lists of relevant hypotheses submitted to him by scientists, then by observing this last rule we would all end up in selecting specific hypotheses in all areas of inquiry. And, of course, anyone can think of an indefinite number of similar rules which will equally well do the required job.

This objection may quickly be disposed of. Just as the adequacy of a hypothesis is of decisive importance so is the adequacy of the guiding rules to hypothesis selection. An adequate hypothesis, we said, was one selected according to the useable guiding rule; an adequate guiding rule is one selected according to the useable guiding rule for the selecting of guiding rules to the selection of hypotheses. The rule for the selection of hypotheses just referred to suggested that we employ information extra to the observational results to be accounted for; in particular information concerning the choice of the V.P. There are indefinitely many such rules, e.g., 'select the hypothesis designated by Queen Elizabeth'. Thus if our metaguiding rule is 'use the guiding rule employing no information additional to the observations to be accounted for by our hypotheses', then we are led to the rule 'select the hypothesis postulating the most parsimonious equation'. But if our meta-guiding rule is 'use the guiding rule which employs information additional to the observations to be accounted for by our hypothesis' then we are led to no specific guiding rule.

Firstly, because of the all pervasive importance of Principle A, and secondly because to my knowledge it has not been explicitly advanced by any one else, I think it will be useful if we dwell on it a little further. Some twenty years after Jeffreys, Nelson Goodman has come up with what he has called 'the new problem of induction'. In fact his problem is essentially the same as Jeffreys', namely that given any finite number of observations, there are always infinitely many ways to account for them, each description resulting in a different claim as to what law has been governing the phenomena under observation, and consequently leading to different hypotheses concerning the course of future events. Goodman presents his problem in the following way: suppose we define

> Grue = observed before the year 2000 A.D. and found green or observed after the year 2000 A.D. and found blue.

It is obvious that all our past observations concerning the color of emeralds permit us to say that all emeralds have been grue no less than that all emeralds have been green. If, however, we describe our experiences as having observed that all emeralds were grue, and assume this to be true in the future as well, then we expect emeralds to look different after 2000 A.D. than we would expect if we subscribed to 'All emeralds are green'.

A large number of solutions have been suggested. Goodman's own solution is that there is a methodological principle according to which, of all the possible predicates which we could apply to the subjects under investigation, we must treat only the predicate which is entrenched in our language as 'projectible'. Therefore, since the predicate 'green' is entrenched in the language whereas 'grue' is not, the hypothesis 'All emeralds are green' is projectible while 'All emeralds are grue' is not.

Goodman confines himself to stating it as a fact that everybody regards it as natural to use entrenched predicates only; he makes no attempt to defend this principle. I should like to point out, however, that if indeed the question should arise whether (a) we should use entrenched predicates only in our projections or (b) we may (or should) use unentrenched predicates, then by just once more applying Principle A we arrive at the conclusion that (a) must be adopted. For in the case where we accept (a), then in a situation where we have made a large number of observations concerning the color of emeralds, the only entrenched predicate we find applicable to our past experiences is 'green' and we are therefore led to the choice of the specific hypothesis 'All emeralds are green'. If however we adopted (b) then we should not end up with the choice of any specific hypothesis. There are, after all, infinitely many unentrenched predicates such as 'grue$_1$', which is defined like 'grue' except that '2001 A.D.' replaces '2000 A.D.', and 'grue$_2$', and so on. (b) provides us with no instruction whether we should select 'All emeralds are grue$_1$' or 'All emeralds are grue$_2$', or what.

Just one more important illustration. The most central of the methodological rules of science has often been said to be: assume that the unobserved will be like the observed. An alternative to this has been described in the literature and referred to as 'counter-induction'. This rule bids us to assume that the unobserved will be unlike the observed. Why do we not subscribe to counter-induction? Some people have thought that the answer is that it leads us to contradictory hypotheses and we can reject on *a priori* grounds any rule which leads us to the choice of contradictory hypotheses. Max Black, for example, says:

Suppose we were using [counter-induction] to predict the terms of a series of 1's and 0's of which the first three terms were known to be 1's. Then our first two predictions might be as follows 1 1 1 0 0. At this point suppose [counter-induction] has been used successfully in each of the two predictions, so that the series is in fact now observed to be 1 1 1 0 0. Since 1's still predominate, direct application of this rule calls for o to be predicated next. On the other hand, the second-order argument shows that [counter-induction] has been successful each time and therefore demands that it not be trusted next time, i.e., calls for prediction of 1. So the very definition of [counter-induction] renders it impossible for the rule to be successful without being *incoherent*.[3]

Black seems to have exaggerated the difficulty facing counter-induction. First of all, in the situation described by him it could be quite reasonable to maintain that in view of the enormous number of failures counter-induction has had in the past, it is still correct to say that this method has, on the whole, been unsuccessful in the past and therefore it is bound to be successful in the next instance and we predict 0. In addition, it may also be maintained that the counter-induction method is to be applied only to the regularities found among natural phenomena but not to the method itself. Consequently no matter how successful counter-induction has been in the past, we are not obligated to argue that in the next instance it will be unsuccessful.

But the correct reason why we cannot adopt counter-induction as our hypothesis-selection-rule is because it does not lead us to the choosing of a specific hypothesis. This becomes evident as soon as we consider a situation of the kind in which we have observed that the law that has been governing the correlation

[3] 'Self-Supporting Inductive Arguments' in *The Philosophy of Science*, ed. P. M. Nidditch (Oxford, 1968) pp. 142–3.

between two physical parameters x and y can be described by $y = f(x)$, since all the hitherto observed values of x and y have satisfied $y = f(x)$. Adopting counter-induction as our method commits us to postulating that the law to be obeyed in the future will be described by a different equation. But there are infinitely many different equations and we are given no clue which one to choose. Does the rule perhaps imply that we adopt the equation which differs *most* from $y = f(x)$? How do we produce this particular equation? Are we to say that if $y = f(x)$ consisted of n terms, the equation we are after has infinitely many terms? Surely the equation maximally different from $y = f(x)$ is unobtainable. But perhaps we should say that the equation we are looking for is minimally different from $y = f(x)$. Should we then say, perhaps, that the required equation is identical in form with $y = f(x)$ but differs with respect to the values of one of the co-efficients? But the coefficient of which term? And it differs by how much? And is the difference positive or negative? It seems, therefore, that the only feasible conclusion to arrive at on the basis of counter-induction is that whatever the equation representing the co-variation of x and y, it is different from $y = f(x)$. But this is not a useable hypothesis in the sense that it would not yield even a single concrete prediction as to the value of y for any specific value of x. Thus, if we picked a particular function g and maintained, on the basis of counter-induction, that while hitherto $y = f(x)$ represented the co-variation of x and y, in the future $y = g(x)$ will do so, this would not be an adequate hypothesis, since we would not have been led to it specifically by the guiding rule we use. It is only when we use straight induction in conjunction with Jeffreys' principle and Goodman's principle that we reach a specific hypothesis.

IV

Suppose everyone agreed that all that I have said concerning

Principle A was true. Would we then have a justification of scientific method? On the one hand, of course, we would have a very compelling reason to adhere to the methodology we currently use. It would, after all, be absurd to want to replace any rule belonging to this methodology with some other rule of hypothesis-selection which did not lead to the selection of any determinate hypothesis. Given that we must act in one way or in another, then even if we have no way of securing the truth, it is still preferable to have some hypothesis which sanctions a given line of action to having no hypothesis and be provided with no clue as to how to act. However, when we have chosen a hypothesis in accordance with scientific method, we do not merely think that what we have achieved is a definite direction how to act; our attitude is one of very strong trust that the predictions based on our hypothesis are very likely to be true. Thus the problem arises that our way of justifying the tenets of empirical reasoning provides only a basis for actually subscribing to those tenets, but not for the confidence which normally accompanies their use.

We see, then, that the task of justifying the use of scientific method and the task of explaining our trust in its results are two separate tasks. A hypothesis may, after all be adopted with two different views in mind. Firstly, one may hold that a hypothesis concerning the laws of nature serves as a basis for providing us with information on how to act. In other words, a scientific hypothesis implying that an act a has the consequence c may in essence be treated as an instruction: act as if you know that a has the consequence c. Another way of treating a hypothesis is to regard it as actually representing the truth. Now while our principle clearly sanctions only the adoption of a hypothesis in so far as it instructs us with regard to our behavior, in actual fact we have very strong confidence that these hypotheses express the truth. The question which remains to be answered is: why is it that when the hypothesis we are lead to adopt by the rules of scientific methodology implies that an act a brings about c, where c is a highly dreaded consequence, then we do not simply refrain from doing *a*, but recoil from *a* with an intense feeling of horror?

The answer to this question might be found upon realizing that, even prior to all experience, we make certain fundamental presuppositions concerning the nature of the universe. It has often been maintained that science is based on certain metaphysical presuppositions concerning the form and character of nature's laws. Among the more famous of these is the presupposition that every event must have a cause, or the more specific assertion that effects have causes which resemble them, or that effects must be contiguous with their causes, or the less far-going claim that nature is uniform in some sense. It is by no means at once obvious why human beings should have been strongly motivated to hold any of these ideas. But there is one presupposition, often referred to in the literature, which is perhaps the most modest in its scope among all the alleged presuppositions and for which one can very easily offer an explanation of why people should have wanted to believe in it. This is the principle of the intelligibility of nature, according to which, nature's laws are not of such a character as to place them beyond the capacity of the human mind to comprehend them. Without any legthy elaboration, it is obvious why a belief that nature will be found amenable to our investigations and is, so to speak, 'friendly' rather than forbidding and to be forever shrouded in mystery, is a comforting belief.

Now it is obvious that while a belief in the intelligibility of nature would have provided general encouragement, filling us with optimism that eventually we are going to unravel nature's mysteries, such a belief, on its own, would have done nothing to enlighten us about the specific form of the laws we should be looking for. In fact, any law is compatible with this belief as long as it is not so complicated as to forever lie beyond human comprehension, that is as long as it is not of the kind which we would not be looking for anyhow. Also, when it comes to the question of which methods of investigation we should use, it is not clear what specific method the principle of the intelligibility of nature sanctions. Surely it could not be claimed that any method we should be happening to use will elicit from nature its secrets, since different methods supposedly lead to contrary hypotheses. But now we are in the position to realize that this seemingly innocuous presupposition is of the utmost significance and it provides us with what we are after. If nature is intelligible, then it must yield its secrets to our investigations. We need no longer wonder: yes, but to what kind of investigations? We now realize that there is but one set of rules which leads to determinate hypotheses and which is thus useable at all. If nature is to respond to our investigations conducted by some set of rules, it is inevitable that she should respond to the rules which we are obliged to use. Thus the principle of the intelligibility of nature implies that the set of rules constituting scientific method is such that one can rely upon it to produce truth.

But it may still be objected that even after producing a justification for the employment of the methodology, we do employ an explanation as to why we believe in its efficacy to produce true hypotheses, and we do not seem to have a justification for our belief. The principle of the intelligibility of nature may be a very modest and a very appealing principle but it is by no means self-evidently true.

An attempt may be made to reply to this that grounds have already been provided upon which to justify our belief in the efficacy of our methodology to produce true hypotheses. After all, it has been demonstrated that the standards of reasonability demand that we adhere to the current methods of science. By definition of the term 'reasonable' or 'rational', the fact that a given hypothesis has been selected by a rule that it is rational or reasonable to have adopted, renders it inevitably reasonable or rational to have confidence that it will lead to correct predictions. What we have here then is a Strawsonian kind of justification which, however, has been strongly reinforced. As is well-known,

Strawson said that by the rules of the language we call it reasonable to have confidence in induction since induction provides good and reliable grounds — by virtue of the definition of 'good and reliable grounds' — for believing the conclusions it leads to. Strawson's suggestion has been recognized as very important and differs profoundly from the kind of attempts made before him to justify scientific method. Yet his suggestion is open to one powerful objection, namely that he does not provide an answer to the question why in the first place it is an accepted convention to regard the rules of induction as reasonable, and reliable means by which one may be assured to arrive at the truth? And if he has no answer to this question we may well wonder whether if some other set of rules had been adopted by us as our tool to produce empirical hypotheses, then automatically we would have conferred rationality and reliability upon these rules? As a result of these questions, one cannot escape the feeling that according to the view held by Strawson, the terms 'rational', 'good grounds' and so on have lost their very substance as they are not rooted in any way in objective reality but spring from seemingly entirely arbitrary conventions.

Now, however, there is no longer any room for these misgivings. It is by no means an arbitrary convention to adopt the rules of induction as our hypothesis-selection-rules. Objective reality demands that we do so since it follows from the nature of things that these are the only useable rules. The question, therefore, whether if some other set of rules had been adopted by us, then we would have automatically conferred rationality and reliability upon these rules, does not arise. We simply could not have adopted any other set of rules to produce for us the hypotheses we adopt.

In other words, the question before us was, in the case where scientific methodology currently in use bids me to adopt hypothesis-selection-rule r, which leads me to the selection of h implying that if I do a then c is to happen, where c is a disastrous

event, is there an objective justification for me to recoil with
actual fear from doing a? The answer that I have suggested here
is this: it has been demonstrated that reason plainly demands that
we adopt r. It is also a fact that r directs us to subscribe to h as an
hypothesis. It is reasonable therefore that I accept h. h however
asserts that c inevitably follows a, and c is a fearsome event. It is
reasonable therefore not by mere definition, but in the sense that
it inevitably follows from the nature of things that it is reasonable,
to fear that by doing a I shall bring about c.

CHAPTER 22

MIRACLES

I

Now we are in a position to give a clear account of the status of a miraculous event which is the most conspicuous candidate for constituting possible confirmatory evidence in support of Theism. It seems that most people would be prepared to admit that a major miracle, announced ahead of time by a generally acknowledged religious figure (someone with an impeccable moral character, who is most of the time engaged in one kind of religious activity or another and so on), occurring at the right moment, resulting in rescuing and greatly promoting the welfare of the righteous who are known to believe firmly in God and proclaim his name and in the defeat of palpably wicked idolaters, would strongly indicate the existence of Divine power and providence. The reason, of course, why recorded miracles fail to impress many people greatly nowadays is because they are skeptical as to whether such happenings ever took place. Hume, for instance, provides strong reasons why the accounts of miraculous events should not be trusted. At least part of the point of his argument is to convince people that they need not regard Theism as confirmed to any degree by these happenings, since there is good reason for saying that they never took place.

Each of the ten plagues brought down upon Egypt may be regarded as a major miracle with the power to induce people to believe in God. If conclusive evidence could be produced that their story, as recorded in Exodus and embellished by the Midrash, was literally true to the last detail, many an agnostic would be prepared to reconsider the force of the theistic claim. By literally true to the last detail I mean that, for instance, in the case of the first plague all the waters of Egypt except those in the province of Goshen, at once turned into actual blood (and not merely muddy waters resembling blood) after Moses had explicitly warned that God would make this happen and at the very moment when Aaron struck the water that was in the Nile. Let us not worry now about the fact that conclusive evidence for the truth of such a story is perhaps, in principle, impossible and try to imagine what would happen if we were really entirely convinced that it was true. It seems to me that most of us would think that Theism was supported by quite impressive evidence. Now I shall offer an explanation why.

Let P stand for the statement that the story of the ten plagues as specified before is true. We shall treat P as an observation statement in the sense that we shall consider it as unquestionably true. Let T stand for the theistic hypothesis and N for the naturalistic hypotheses. P of course, does not logically imply T. P, however, strongly tends to confirm T as compared to N by Principle E since given T, P is much more probable than when N is given. It will, after all, be agreed that given the naturalistic hypothesis, such extraordinary events are highly unlikely to happen, while given that God exists it is by no means improbable that when an intensely pious person specifies the spectacular way God will punish those who defy him in spite of several warnings, then the occurrence described by such a man — no matter how unprecedented — will take place. I am not saying that given T the probability of P is one. It cannot be maintained that if T is true then a miracle to help the righteous and punish the wicked is bound to happen and indeed, we can recall many instances in which such a miracle failed to materialize. However, it is reasonable to assert that if an omnipotent and omnibenevolent God does exist then the more clearly the lines are drawn between the virtuous and the sinful, that is, the less ambiguity exists as to who stands clearly for God and who stands against him, and the more outstanding the religious credentials of the person who prophesies that a miracle is about to occur, the higher the probability that such an event will indeed take place. Thus there is a difference between the probability that the events recorded in Exodus should have taken place on T than on N and that is why by Principle E these events confirm T.

In order to avoid misunderstanding I should like to emphasize that I do not deny that one could invent indefinitely many reasons why even someone who held T to be true, could not be sure that the miracles announced by Moses are actually going to take place. Perhaps God wants to test the faithful's resolve to continue to hold on to their belief in spite of God's failure to do anything for them; perhaps it is contrary to Divine plans to help the righteous in this world since they will have sufficient compensation in the world to come, and so on. All this is not very important. The relevant question to ask is this: Admittedly the ways of God are not wholly scrutable. Yet, suppose there were two people t and n, the first being a firm theist, the other a naturalist; when they heard Moses' announcement, did they regard the fulfillment of his fantastic prophecy as improbable to exactly the same degree? It would seem that the answer is no. Admittedly t could think of many reasons why the prophecy may fail to materialize but he also has some quite weighty positive reasons, which to n of course do not exist, why it is going to be fulfilled. It is reasonable therefore to assume that t expects P to become true somewhat more strongly than n. This is sufficient for our purposes.

I should also like to point out that my purpose is to argue that the kind of miracles under discussion confirm T. I take it that most people are willing to concede this. The following statement made very recently is, I believe, typical of the position generally held:

However in this world the gods do not appear in a publicly verifiable form high in the sky, giving loud predictions and performing miracles in accordance with those predictions, hence religious belief-claims cannot be established by scientific criteria.[1]

That is, it is taken for granted, which is often ruefully expressed by agnostics, that we should be very lucky if we lived in a world in which major miracles, announced in advance by God (through his messengers or, for that matter, through a voice from heaven) did take place. Then we would not need to live with any nagging doubts, for then Theism would be confirmed. My purpose in this chapter is to show that the admitted confirmation would come about through the use of the elementary principles of scientific method that apply in general.

II

It is important, however, to realize that in the confirmation of T, Principle A also plays a role. Suppose someone advances the following fanciful hypothesis. There is a powerful demon who is very malicious. In his wickedness this demon severely punishes, in the after-life, all those who entertain such noble beliefs as that a benevolent Divine Being exists. Being even more wicked he wants to have the opportunity to torment people in hell, so he does all sorts of things to convince them that God does exist. Let D denote the hypothesis that such a demon exists and rules the world. P is no less probable on the basis of D than it is on the basis of T. Principle E provides no reason why we should not regard D rather than T as confirmed by the occurrences of the plagues. In other words while Principle E can be employed to defeat some of the rivals of T, in particular N, it does not weaken at all the appeal of D. Indeed, the reason why most of us would opt for T rather than for D is not because we are able to interpret P as being more indicative of the truth of T than of D. In fact no experience is conceivable that would indicate more the truth of T than that of

[1] Frank B. Dilley, 'The Status of Religious Beliefs', *American Philosophical Quarterly* (1976), p. 41.

D. It is simply that D is deemed as intrinsically less adequate a hypothesis than T. D is regarded as altogether too 'strange' a hypothesis to have an appeal. Thus D is rejected because of Principle A,[2] while N, which on its own, does not seem unreasonable, loses credibility in comparison with T because of Principle E.

It should also be pointed out that the confirmatory power of P with respect to T does not reside in the fact that P refers to events of which it has been conclusively shown that they are contrary to the laws of nature. Suppose in the course of time, it is discovered that water molecules, which ultimately consist of the same kind of elementary particles as blood cells, under very special circumstances, through a process triggered by a very unusual kind of combination of radiations and by interacting with their surroundings, have their ultimate constituents rearranged into blood cells. It is also discovered that the right confluence of factors which of natural necessity causes such a transmutation and which on the average materializes once every ten billion years at some place on the surface of the earth, has occurred in Egypt in all those places in which water has turned into blood at exactly the time Aaron stretched out his arm. I do not think that such a discovery would in any way weaken our inclination to regard T as confirmed. Having a completely naturalistic account of the kind just outlined of the great miracle should not diminish its power to impress us. For let L be the large set of all the very complicated laws of nature which play a role in the transmutation in question and also the large set — consisting of hundreds of statements — describing the initial conditions which are required for such a transmutation. L would of course now be known to be true, but were we given N alone, which says that there is nothing behind the laws of nature and that the initial physical conditions are what they are for no further reason, L would be very improbable. Given

---

[2] This will be discussed at great length in the next chapter.

that there are infinitely many sets of laws which could have
governed the universe and the infinitely many initial conditions
which could have prevailed, the likelihood that, in fact, L will
apply is viewed as having been very minute, if N – which is
symmetrically related to all those sets – had, in fact, been the true
hypothesis. On T however, it is more probable, of course, that the
Divine Creator of the universe, who is the author of its laws and
the arranger of all the initial conditions in it, will see to it that L
obtains.

The effectiveness of a miracle to render theism more credible
derives then from something other than the fact that it represents
a physically impossible event. In fact to say, as is sometimes said,
that a miracle is a physically impossible event is both unnecessary
and insufficient. What is essential for an event to count as miraculous is that it be an event whose occurrence, without knowing
that the laws of nature and the initial conditions require it, is more
probable on assuming T to be true than on assuming any reasonable rival of T to be true. If this condition is fulfilled then it makes
no difference that the event in question is, in fact, a natural event.
On the other hand, if an event does not seem at all more probable
on the assumption that T is true than on the assumption that any
of the contraries of T is true, then the fact that the event is con-
tary to the laws of nature does not render it miraculous.

III

It will be instructive to consider briefly a recent discussion of Kai
Nielsen of a situation which bears some resemblance to the one
discussed here. He considers a hypothetical situation in which all
sick people who pray with their whole heart to God recover no
matter how incurable their disease had been pronounced before.
The recovery rate among all those sick people who do not pray
sincerely does not improve at all. This continues for a long period
and there is no scientific account available – for some reason there

is not even any plausible psychosomatic account for what is going on. The theist would want to take this as evidence for the existence of a God who answers prayers, while the naturalist would refuse to do so. The naturalist would admit that he finds this fantastic situation baffling and that at present he has no explanation for it at all. But says Nielsen:

Maybe he never will have, but it seems to me, he would be right in asserting that he sees no reason for saying that in principle there can be no naturalistic explanation of such events.[3]

It is possible that Nielsen holds on *a priori* grounds that Theism is so much inferior to Naturalism, that when arguing against religion one need not adhere to the standards of scientific method which apply when the relative confirmation of two hypotheses is considered. Otherwise his reasoning is unacceptable. If it were acceptable then the adherent of the flat-earth theory can also claim that there is no reason why he should abandon his cherished belief about the shape of the earth. True enough at the moment there are quite a number of phenomena which fit very well the round-earth hypothesis and for which at present he has no explanation at all. Maybe he never will have, but surely no proof has yet been produced to show that, in principle, these phenomena cannot perfectly well be accounted for by the flat-earth hypothesis. But of course, we would reject his argument by saying that if indeed it should turn out that on the flat-earth hypothesis, we could just as well account for the phenomena, which at the moment we cannot, and it is taken now to indicate the roundness of the earth, then we should certainly review our attitude. But before that happens we shall resolutely keep upholding the round-earth hypothesis. Since empirical hypotheses are not in general conclusively proven to be false, one must always bear in mind the possibility that new

[3] 'Empiricism, Theoretical Constructs and God', *The Journal of Religion* (1974), p. 200.

evidence might arise to vindicate a hypothesis now disconfirmed or that we succeed in constructing an acceptable theory in the context of which the currently hostile evidence to our disconfirmed hypothesis is neutralized. But it does not mean that because of the possibility that the tide may turn in favour of a currently discredited hypothesis, we never discard a hypothesis even if nothing has yet happened to vindicate it.

What Nielsen could have claimed with much greater plausibility is that Theism is not an adequate account of the extraordinary happenings since it cannot be claimed that given T it is very probable that those people who pray will recover. After all, past experience does not bear out the claim that prayers are always answered and hence even Theists have reconciled themselves to the fact that often God does not grant our petitions.

It is still interesting to consider for a moment the position of a theist who interprets God's benevolence to imply that really sincere prayers of a deserving person may produce results. On this interpretation of Theism the events described by Nielsen should be regarded somewhat more probable on T than on N. But in that case, it should be emphasized, those events support the credibility of T as compared to N, not only when the naturalist has no account to offer for what is going on but even if it should turn out that the recovery of the praying invalids can be explained naturalistically. Suppose we discover a law L which asserts that whenever a person is engaged in sincere prayer in the way the people in Nielsen's story have been engaged, he induces in himself a unique state of mind which is invariably associated with a very specific state of the brain that is both sufficient and necessary for triggering the defense mechanism of his body which when activated, is capable of overcoming any disease. Suppose we even fully understand the physical and chemical mechanism underlying L. What we have to consider is the question: when we did not know of the existence of L nor of the phenomena described by Nielsen, how probable was it then that, in fact, there be such a law as L which ensures that the happening referred to will indeed take place? Now while it has to be conceded that even if theism is true it is by no means a certainty that there be actually a law like L, it would still have to be admitted that the existence of L is more probable on the theistic hypothesis than on the naturalistic hypothesis. The very discovery of L therefore constitutes confirmatory evidence which supports Theism rather than Naturalism.

CHAPTER 23

THE EVIDENCE FOR THEISM

I

Now we shall once more look at the claim that there is evidence, the existence of which is unquestioned, which supports the credibility of Theism. This claim may be presented in a number of ways. For example, it is unquestionably true that human beings exist who possess awareness and conscience and are capable of a wide range of emotions and sentiments. It is also undisputedly true that the laws of nature which govern the universe, and the initial conditions, are such that complex and precarious systems like humans can come into existence and survive. Human beings are creatures who are capable of responding to the Divine. By this I mean that they have the potential for acknowledging and contemplating God, as well as having feelings of awe and love toward him. Humans are capable of moral judgements and they have the capacity to feel, and nurture in themselves the feeling of compassion, humility, courage, forbearance and similar morally, hence religiously, desirable sentiments. They are also capable of acting according to these sentiments. Let T stand once more for the theistic hypothesis which, among others, contains the statement that God, who is interested in creatures capable of responding to him, exists. Let R state that the laws of nature governing the universe and the initial conditions in it are such that creatures capable of responding to the Divine are permitted to exist. It is clear that from T alone, one can derive that there is a universe and that this universe is such that the conditions prevailing in it allow the existence of some sort of creatures similar to man. That is, while the essence of Theism is merely the claim that the universe was willed by a Perfect Being, yet, since the more benevolence the more perfection, it is implied that the Being is Omnibenevolent. It is not unreasonable to maintain that Omnibenevolence implies the wish that there be creatures capable of contemplating the Divine and lead a God-centered life. Thus by T, there is a God who is interested in such creatures, and being all-powerful — therefore capable of realizing anything he wishes — it follows that such creatures must exist.[1] Given, however, N instead, which in essence is the claim that there are no super-natural forces, that the physical universe and its laws are whatever they are, not as a result of a transcendent being who willed them into existence, then it is by no means the case that the existing universe had to be just the way it is. All sorts of universes are conceivable and we can easily postulate a great number of them in which human beings did not exist. Consider a universe in which nothing existed but three electrons. Such a universe, which is so easily described, is quite compatible with N. It is obvious that we could go on describing any number of universes in which nothing like humans existed or were even allowed to exist by the laws governing those universes. Given nothing more than just N, it does not follow that the actual universe is not a member of the infinitely large set of universes in which no human-like creatures come into being.

What I just said does not mean that I hold that a naturalist may not have a very compelling explanation why humans should be driven by a strong urge to invent and worship a non-existent God. But as I have indicated in Part II, N *per se* is confined to the assertion that nothing exists apart from the physical universe.

---

[1] It may perhaps seem incorrect that everything God is interested in happening is ensured to happen. He is interested, for instance, that everyone be virtuous and yet some people are not. But, of course, given that God wants humans to possess freedom of the will, it follows logically that it is impossible for him to make certain that they always act virtuously. It may, however, be safely asserted that anything logically possible for him to do, if God wants to bring it about, is ensured to happen.

Thus N as such implies nothing about human nature; it does not even imply that creatures resembling humans in any way exist.

It follows, therefore, that by Principle E, the very fact that the actual universe is the way it is, namely, that in the existing universe R happens to be true, confirms T as compared to N. The reason is because $p(R/T) > p(R/N)$. We need not give any sophisticated account of the technical concept of probability; and without going into any of the numerous interpretations of that notion, but merely taking a most simple-minded attitude, it is abundantly clear that something that must be the case is more likely to be the case than something that need not be the case. It goes without saying that it makes no difference to statements that are known to be true whether they are necessarily true or only contingently so; their probability is one. But I am, of course, talking about the probability of R in the context of a complete absence of observations. But as we have already said, given nothing but that T is true, it is already certain that R must be true, whereas given no empirical propositions whatever, and all we know is that N is true, then it does not follow that R must be true. No more is required in order to see clearly that the assertion that $p(R/T) > p(R/N)$ is true.

I shall indicate extremely briefly another way of advancing the claim that there is evidence favoring T. It could be pointed out that the existing universe could contain beings who were in many ways similar to humans, who possessed intelligence, awareness and the potential for contemplating the Divine. These beings, however, were physically prevented from carrying out any act in accordance with a theistic belief; they were not even able to utter any statement affirming their belief in God. There is nothing in N to rule out that the actual universe was not inhabited by this kind of religiously paralysed being instead of the humans we now know to exist. However T, which states that the universe is governed by an omnibenevolent being and which implies that devotion to religious activities, which renders a man's life infinitely more valuable than it otherwise would be, implies that the universe is not inhabited by beings who have the potential to achieve a valuable life but are frustrated from actually achieving it. But in the actual universe we find fully fledged humans rather than such pitiable creatures. This confirms T as compared to N.

II

At this stage we shall look at some arguments why T may be said to be more confirmed than any D-like hypothesis, which also concedes that there is some being behind the universe which willed it and its laws into existence, but that that being is different from the God of Theism.

Before doing so I should like to emphasize that it is not very crucial that I should be successful with my arguments. The fact is that, what has always been regarded as of paramount importance among philosophers of religion is whether or not it is possible to produce proof of evidence that would adjudicate between T and N. It is N, and not any D-like hypothesis, which has been taken in the last few hundred years to constitute the real threat to T. The numerous objections to the Argument from Design, for example, are all directed toward showing that there is no reason to claim that N may not account just as well for the existing state of affairs. The objections do not point out what they could have pointed out, that if the state of the world could be said to support T it could just as well be said to support D. Nor does Hume, in his vigorous attacks on the arguments from miracles, stress that if miracles did take place then these would support D no less than T. Nor again does Nielsen, who is anxious to argue that the events described by him need not embarrass anyone holding N, bother to point out that these events are relevant to D exactly as they are relevant to T, and so on indefinitely.

The situation is much more favorable here than it was with respect to Pascal. Pascal's Wager not only fails to provide an argument against D but also provides no support for any particular brand of Theism. Now in his case, this may be construed as a drawback which may result in not having reached any useful conclusion at all. For even if it is agreed that, of all the supernatural forces which are candidates for having authored the universe, T is by far the most superior, it may still be claimed that his argument leads nowhere. The reason is that he argues, not for the credibility of any proposition, but for accepting a certain set of rules of behavior. But different brands of Theism prescribe contrary sets of rules of behavior. Not being given any guidance as to which particular set to adopt, we are practically where we were without his argument. Here, however, we are arguing for the credibility of T and if we agree that T is the only viable supernatural explanation, then we have achieved a great deal. Even before being provided with any clue as to which brand of Theism is most credible, just knowing that T as such is credible is to have acquired substantial knowledge.

Now to the arguments why T may be said to be more confirmed than any D-like hypothesis. What reasons could one expect would be given by those who regard it quite natural that if the choice is restricted to hypotheses which postulate the will of a supernatural agent as the ultimate origin of the universe, then T must be selected? One line of reasoning that might be envisaged would make reference to the existence of arguments which uniquely support T against any hypothesis which postulates an alternative agent. Perhaps the most fascinating of all these is the famous ontological argument. This argument is based essentially on the idea of the perfection of God and that, by definition, he is a being than which none greater can be conceived, and claims that by virtue of this unique aspect of God it is self-contradictory to assert that he does not exist. I shall not state this famous argument for which there exist so many different versions and with the basic outlines of which everyone is familiar, but note that because of the central role that the notion of perfection plays in it, it cannot be applied to argue that logic requires the existence of an all powerful but morally defective demon.

This may not be evident at once because of the first and foremost objection, due to Gaunilo, that a Lost Island which excells all the lands that men inhabit, is intelligible and hence, it too must, by the argument, exist. This objection seems, on the surface, very effective and was often repeated throughout history; in our century by B. Russell[2] who also claimed that by following the lines of the ontological argument one can think into existence just about everything. Bonaventura,[3] however, seems to have looked somewhat deeper into this matter and has come up with what appears to be the correct answer to this objection. What he says is, in essence, that it is vital to the ontological argument that its subject is a being to whom we wish to assign perfection in every respect. One cannot intelligibly predicate such perfection to an island which is intrinsically defective, e.g., must be limited in space — the concept of an island of infinite area is a self-contradictory notion. Similarly, a demon who might be perfect with respect to the amount of power it possessed but was morally depraved would be, on the whole, imperfect and the ontological argument could not apply to it.

The theist is thus greatly impressed by the fact that such an extraordinary, i.e., many-faceted argument which employs logic alone to establish the existence of a real being, has been attempted in such a great variety of manners by so many people. Of course he is aware of the fact that many have claimed to have discovered flaws in the argument. One of the most famous of such claims is due to Kant. He argued that the ontological argument hinges on the assumption that existence is a predicate and obeys the logic of normal predicates, an assumption which he shows to be false.

---

[2] 'On Denoting', *Mind* (1905).
[3] Cited in J. Hick and A. McGill, *The Many Faced Argument* (London, 1968), p. 24.

While many have regarded his attack as conclusive, there are others who have tried to show with considerable cogency that the ontological argument does not require the assumption discredited by Kant.[4] But there were also other objections, each in turn giving rise to many rejoinders. Lately, with the development of modal logic, many new versions have sprung up which their authors have thought were immune to the attack to which earlier verisons were subjected.

The significant point in all this is that a theist might contend that it is practically impossible for anyone to have fully mastered all the claims and counter-claims that have been made and are possible to make concerning this many-faceted set of arguments that are reconstructions of, derive from, or are inspired by, the original ontological argument. At least, not to the extent of being able to hand down a judgement that all the arguments in this family of arguments are, beyond doubt, doomed to complete failure. St. Anselm seems to have discovered a many-layered mine from which philosophers have kept extracting a great variety of arguments that differ from one another with respect to the ease with which their value may be assessed. Now of course, it may be the case that any argument that may be constructed modelling St. Anselm's argument, will eventually be proven beyond doubt entirely useless. But there is at least a slight possibility that this may not be the case. In fact, it would seem that the issue is not whether or not some plain logical blunder is committed in each one of the possible arguments, but rather, in many cases at least, whether certain assumptions are reasonable. The various versions of the ontological argument make different presuppositions concerning, for instance, the correct meaning of the term 'perfection' or 'necessary existence'; and the question is to what extent these presuppositions are binding as required by some of these versions or are just plausible, as required by others. Once

---

[4]   e.g., A. Plantinga, *op. cit.*, pp. 29–47.

more it may be that all the assumptions underlying the various versions of the ontological argument are inadmissible. But at least it is arguable that there is a slight probability that some of these are not entirely unreasonable. This small probability lends T a unique advantage from the very start.[5]

Another argument the Theist might advance, showing why, for him, T has enough initial plausibility to at least qualify as a plausible rival for N and thus set up a contest in which Principle E is to determine the hypothesis to be adopted, is from tradition. He finds it remarkable that there are wide-spread and long-held traditions concerning the occurrence of a variety of miraculous events supportive of T. He is, of course, aware that the occurrence of these events has by no means been established historically, yet the very existence of these events actually took place, to be slightly more than zero.

It may be objected that, in fact, it need not be assumed that the probability of events, supportive of Theism and which have widely been believed to have occurred, is of a finite value since the fact that a belief in their occurrence has taken such firm roots in people's minds can fully be accounted for psychologically. The existence of a very powerful, wise and just being who can be relied upon to protect us and who provides proper management to the universe and sees to it that ultimately justice prevails, is something we all greatly yearn for and hence, there is ample motivation to bring him into being through imagining all sorts of events pointing to his existence.

The Theist's reply to this is that it is by no means clear in which direction wishful thinking is more liable to take us. One can offer many good reasons why we human beings should naturally prefer

[5] Of course there have also been some attempts to disprove logically the existence of God, e.g., J. N. Findlay in *Language of Mind and Value* (London, 1963), pp. 96–104. Such isolated instances, however, are overwhelmingly outnumbered by the plethora of arguments claiming to demonstrate with the aid of logic alone the existence of God.

a state of affairs in which we represent the ultimate in power and wisdom, a world in which we are masters of our destiny, in which there are no quotas to fulfil and everything is permitted, where one is never going to be called upon to give a painful accounting of all one's deeds and one need not fear the consequences of one's behaviour, where one can look forward, after one finishes this earthly life, to an absolute rest in peace, which total non-existence amounts to, rather than have to fear a transition into a completely alien form of existence the likes of which have never been experienced before.[6] Thus since both these hypotheses come from speculative psychology, neither of them being supported by rigorously conducted experiments, it is not clear, given human psychology to be what it is, whether it was to be expected that theistic myths should evolve in people's minds or, on the contrary, that this is quite unexpected and hence the existence of belief in these stories is to be pointing toward their origin, at least partially in fact.

Thus, the theist would not treat the various proofs that have been offered for Theism in general or the vast number of versions of the ontological proof in particular, with their different presuppositions, as conclusive or even as rendering Theism considerably probable. Nor would he look upon traditional religious tales as providing such support. What he might claim is that he need not rely entirely on a subjective judgement in deciding to regard T as not being an inadmissible hypothesis to begin with. The arguments cited should be looked upon as lending T at least some objective advantage over hypotheses like D and qualify it to enter into a contest with N.

[6] H. H. Price in his *Essays in the Philosophy of Religion* (Oxford, 1972), pp. 78–97, discusses, for instance, at considerable length the strong psychological motives that there are for a disbelief in life after death and hence the suggestion that the presistent belief in such life may, therefore, have to be accounted for as based on something else rather than on its fulfilling a universally shared wish.

I shall not pass judgement on the arguments just cited and which could be the kind of arguments some might wish to employ. The claim I want to advance is that Principle A, which is the standard principle applied in science to adjudicate between hypotheses that are symmetrically related to all the available evidence, may be employed here too. When it comes to discriminating among the various hypotheses which postulate a transcendent agent as the originator of the universe, the crucial question to be answered is, by what predicate we should describe the agent. Suppose we are given the guiding rule instructing us to select the hypothesis for conferring confirmation upon it, which assigns predicate P to the agent. Suppose further, that following this instruction we postulate that agent has P and thereby arrive at a specific hypothesis postulating a unique agent, for we find that no two non-identical agents may possess P. Lastly, let us also suppose that there is no other rule instructing us to select the hypothesis assigning predicate Q to the agent, where P and Q are incompatible predicates and where no two non-identical agents may possess Q. It is clear that in that case the rule prescribing the selection of the hypothesis assigning P to the agent is an adequate rule and the hypothesis selected by following this rule is an adequate hypothesis, in the technical sense we have defined the term 'adequate'.

What we have to look for then is for proper candidates for P. Suppose we focused on color and asked ourselves what color the agent might have. It is obvious that no matter what answer we received, giving the color of the agent is no help to us in identifying it since many different agents may have exactly the same color.

We would get no further if we tried to describe the agent in terms of the spatial properties it may possess. It makes no difference whether we postulated that the agent occupied a cubic mile or exactly half of the space available in the universe or that he permeated all of space. None of these hypotheses succeeds in providing a unique description of the agent. Once more it is the case that an indefinitely large number of non-identical agents may (logically) have identical spatial properties.

We could go on examining a large number of other candidates for P and find that we would not reach an adequate hypothesis. Suppose, however, we are instructed 'Describe the agent in terms of perfection'. This meta-rule permits an infinite number of guiding rules such as 'Assign to the agent no perfection at all', 'Assign. . .10% perfection', 'Assign. . .90% perfection', 'Assign. . . 100% perfection'. The first rule is out of the question since, if the agent possessed zero perfection, how could he be so enormously powerful as to be created and govern the universe. If we accepted any one of the rules which directed us to assign partial perfection to the agent, we would not be led to a specific hypothesis postulating a unique agent. For example, if the agent was 90% perfect, how should the 10% by which he is short of absolute perfection be deducted; how much should come off his omni-benevolence and how much from his omnipotence? However, the meta rule is useful since it specifically leads to the instruction 'Assign 100% perfection to the agent' because it leads to the singular hypothesis that the agent is God as conceived by Theism. God is uniquely identified by being described as absolutely per-fect, for absolute perfection implies the possession of a singular set of properties including all the Divine attributes.

CHAPTER 24

THEISM AND SCIENTIFIC METHOD

I

What I have claimed then is that by employing the most elementary principles underlying scientific method we may construct certain aspects of the world as constituting empirical evidence confirming Theism. It is conceivable that someone should wish to object saying that Principles A and E, which are admittedly universally employed in the confirmation of scientific hypotheses, are not qualified to adjudicate between hypotheses like T, N, D and so on. Scientific hypotheses postulate that the universe has this but not that feature; that something is, while something else is not, a law of nature; that such and such physical entities, properties, events or processes exist and others do not. The dispute, however, between T and N for instance, is not about what features the universe possesses: T does not deny the existence of any law of nature affirmed by N or *vice versa*; nor are there any physical particulars whose existence is acknowledged by one hypothesis and disavowed by the other. T and N cannot be regarded as empirical hypotheses in the ordinary sense; they are what we typically call metaphysical doctrines. While Principle E is a crucial tool in the confirmation of empirical hypotheses there is no reason to assume that it is correct to employ it in adjudicating between assertions of a radically different kind, namely metaphysical doctrines.

Now while it is by no means required for meeting this objection, it should be emphasized that contrary to what many people believe, it does make a difference to what one expects to be a feature of the physical world whether one accepts T or N. As we have already pointed out, someone who subscribed to T will tend to give much more credence to stories that miracles have occurred than someone who subscribed to N, and miracles are physical events. But circumstances are also conceivable under which a believer in T would be inclined to make different predictions as to what is going to be observed than one who maintained N. Suppose there lived among us a person of intense piety who possessed moral qualities far beyond the ordinary, devoting all his time and prodigious energy to helping others, who on several occasions even risked his life to rescue those in distress, a person who has renounced all worldly pleasures, in sum a person who would universally be regarded a saint. Suppose this man one day proclaims that the day of judgement is at hand and that miraculous events of a specified nature are going to occur on a specified date, which will bespeak of the Lord. An adherent of Naturalism need not assume that the probability that such events are actually going to take place is any greater now than before. In the eyes of the theist, however, the probability that the events predicted by one whom he takes to be a man of God are actually going to happen must be considerably greater than the probability that these events should occur had no such prediction been made. Incidentally, as a consequence of this, should the events in question fail to come about, it would tend to a certain extent to falsify the theistic hypothesis. Thus the holder of T and N will differ in their assessment of the value of the probability of certain events occurring. But differences in assigning values to the probability that certain observable events are going to occur are differences of opinion about matters empirical.

But let me emphasize once more that all this is not needed in order to reply to those who would deny the legitimacy of using Principles A and E to confirm Theism. Let us assume that it makes no difference whatsoever under any conceivable circumstances with respect to the predictions one will be inclined to make or even with respect to tales one will be inclined to believe whether one subscribed to T or N. Let us concede that the questions which scientists ask in the course of their investigations are radically different from the question which does not seek to find out something about any of the yet unknown physical features of the universe, but which asks whether there is anything beyond nature and if so what; this question is still an extremely important question of fact about the universe. It may not be a fact that is important from a practical point of view of how to go about controlling nature and harnessing its forces to our use and consequently some may not wish to know anything about it. Others however, consider this as a most important fact about which they are anxious to find out as much as possible and Principles A and E have been recognized as the major tools in getting to the truth concerning this fact. Now, of course, attempts have been made to deny that a question like 'Does God exist?', which has been categorized as a metaphysical question, can be treated like one would treat an ordinary factual question and the reason given for this denial has been that such questions do not lend themselves to be settled by the usual procedures of empirical confirmation. One cannot, however, legitimately go on in a circle and object to the attempt to claim that Principles A and E, which are at the heart of the usual procedures of empirical confirmation, may properly be employed to adjudicate between T, N and D by asserting that Principles A and E cannot be employed to adjudicate between hypotheses that are not factual!

But really the most important reply is this: I have not merely produced a description of two principles which, as a matter of fact, happen to have been adopted by scientists. I have also justified these principles, demonstrating that Principles A and E are inevitably to be employed when searching for any hypothesis. Once one grasps why they are required, one cannot but realize that it makes no difference what kind of hypothesis we are after, these principles must be the ones which govern the confirmation of all hypotheses. Principle E, we have shown, simply derives from the meaning of 'accounting for' and since Theism purports to account for the origin of the universe and for why everything is the way it is, Principle E necessarily applies when our aim is to investigate whether Theism is confirmed. Principle A must govern any inquiry in which are looking for a determinate hypothesis and surely that is the kind of inquiry we are engaged in when seeking a unique answer to the question why is the universe the way it is.

II

It is clear that the argument I have presented belongs to the same family of arguments which has the famous Argument from Design as its member. I believe that my argument will be found helpful in particular to those who would have been ready to accept the Argument from Design were it not for some of the oft-quoted weighty objections against it. The two best known objections to the classical Argument from Design are, first that it is based on alleged evidence which we are really not entitled to claim to have observed and second that it uses a basically wrong analogy. The first objection denies that one can actually detect a design in the universe, for only when a definite purpose is known to be existing can one speak of something qualifying as possessing the design to fulfill that purpose. The second objection disapproves of the attempt to draw an analogy between objects found within the universe and the universe itself as a whole. Within the universe we know for certain that there exist intelligent agents; we know that there exist objects designed by those agents and others that have not been designed by them; and we have enough experience to teach us how to distinguish between these two kinds of objects. On the other hand, we do not have a number of universes, some designed by intelligent agents, others not so designed; and we have absolutely no experience to go by when trying to distinguish between those two kinds of universe. Thus, we have nothing on the basis of which we could judge, whether the actual universe we live in is designed or undesigned.

No objection, resembling either of these, could be raised against my argument. The evidence on which the argument relies consists of certain well-known aspects of human nature. Nobody would wish to deny the evidence. Neither does the argument draw any analogies between objects within the universe and the universe itself. It is based on the assumption of the validity of two elementary principles which are required to be applied to all instances in which one needs to adjudicate between hypotheses postulating that this or that is the case.

My argument is not vulnerable to the objections which may be raised against a well-known contemporary version of the Argument from Design either. The argument is associated with the name of Lecomte du Noüy and its essence has adequately been rendered by John Rowland:

Evolution purports to explain the emergence of life by some chemical process – a gradual increase in complexity of the molecules. Maybe in outline that is true – but can we say that this occurred by pure chance? Did it happen, somehow, that a series of atoms of carbon, hydrogen and oxygen came together, formed a complex molecule, and that this complex molecule somehow found that it could surround and absorb other molecules – feeding on them, so to speak – so that it was the first little speck of protoplasm? Can we say that?[7]

This clearly amounts to an attempt to employ Principle E to argue for Theism. Life exists, we have clear evidence for that. If T is true then it necessarily follows that life exists. If, however, N is true then there is no reason why life must exist and it only exists because pure chance led to it; life emerged as a result of a highly improbable process of the right elementary particles combining with one another. The fact which constitutes the evidence is required by T but is highly improbable given N instead; the evidence therefore confirms T relative to N.

The basic flaw of this argument is seen as soon as we ask our-

---

[7] *Hibbert Journal* (October, 1961), pp. 3–4.

selves what the evidence is exactly that we are relying on here. Is it the fact that (a) There is life in the universe (L_a)? or (b) There is life on this particular planet (L_b)? Rowland believes that one of these is better accounted for by T, according to which God made certain that there be life, than by N according to which life emerged by pure chance. But surely

$$p(L_a/T) = p(L_a/N) = 1.$$

Since, in our universe with its infinite space and time (or even just immensely vast space and time) even if the emergence of the complex molecules required for life by an entirely unguided random process is very improbable, given the amount of space and time available it is virtually certain to emerge somewhere some time! Consequently even if Naturalism is true, the truth of L_a is ensured.

On the other hand

$$p(L_b/T) = p(L_b/N) \ll 1$$

since even if Theism is true there is nothing in the basic propositions of Theism which would imply that God desires this particular planet to be a place where life emerges.

My argument cannot be attacked along these lines. I am not taking the existing universe, where it is unquestionably true that the laws of nature and the initial conditions are such that they *permit* the emergence of human beings, as given. I am considering the existing universe in the context of all the logically possible universes which certainly include an infinite number of universes where human-like beings at no time exist anywhere. I am, of course, using as my evidence the fact that human beings as we know them exist in our universe (and not the fact that they exist on this particular planet). However, given no information whatever beyond N, it does not follow at all that the universe which actually exists belongs to the class of universes in which human-like creatures are permitted to exist.

III

A word has to be said about the point that Theism is confirmed by the facts that the universe contains beings like humans and that human nature is the way it is. This amounts to no more than that the credibility of Theism, relative to its rivals, is higher than it would be in the absence of these facts. But does it follow that we have to accept Theism as the most credible hypothesis?

The question of the degree of confirmation, provided by a given piece of evidence and the question of how much confirmation is needed to render a hypothesis more credible than its rivals, is a complicated one. However, it may stated that in general a hypothesis which receives more confirmation than its rivals is more credible than its rivals. This implies that if H has received confirmation, no matter of what degree, while none of its rivals have received any confirmation at all, this suffices to render H more confirmed than any of its rivals and therefore more credible than any of its rivals.

Let us consider once more

h_1 = all ravens are black
h_2 = ravens come in a variety of colors
e_1 = of the 5 ravens observed all were black.

Admittedly e_1 by itself is not regarded sufficient to render h_1 more credible than h_2 but that is because there exists other evidence which favors h_2 more than h_1. The fact that it is known that members of other species of birds come in a variety of colors is evidence confirming h_2 rather than h_1. Had it been otherwise, namely if there were no known facts supporting h_2 then it may be claimed that e_1 would have been sufficient to render h_1 credible.

Similarly with

k_1 = our friend is a miracle healer
k_2 = our friend is just an ordinary person
e_2 = our friend when confronted with a person who

has for years been suffering from ulcers, laid
his hands upon the head of that person, who
spontaneously recovered.

Once more it may be claimed that the reason why e_2, which
confirms k_1 relative to k_2, fails to render it more credible than k_2,
is that there is strong prior evidence favoring k_2, namely that in
the past claims about possessing special healing powers have
usually turned out baseless.

Then again, it is also true concerning G, the hypothesis postulating that $s = \frac{1}{2}gt^2$ represents the co-variation of distance and time
for freely falling bodies, that merely one or two experimental
results, which fitted it and therefore confirmed it, would still not
render it credible. The reason here is that before we have a considerable number of results which fit $s = \frac{1}{2}gt^2$ we cannot be very
certain that these results do not also fit some other adequate
hypothesis, namely a hypothesis postulating a different equation
which is not parasitic upon $s = \frac{1}{2}gt^2$ the way, for example, $s =
\frac{1}{2}gt^2 + f_1(x)$ is.

If it is agreed that it is reasonable to hold that when H receives
some confirmation, while its rivals receive none, then H is absolutely more credible than any of its rivals, then we could well
justify the position held by a considerable number of philosophers
concerning the credibility of the claim that other bodies possess a
mind. I refer to those philosophers who accept the so-called
inductive argument. The argument may be presented as follows.
Let

$$l_1 = \text{everybody has a mind}$$
$$l_2 = \text{not everybody has a mind}$$
$$e_3 = \text{I, who have a body, have a mind.}$$

Of course $p(e_3/l_1) > p(e_3/l_2)$ and consequently e_3 confirms
l_1 more than l_2. It has, however, often been objected that this
argument is based on the evidence of a single instance. But those

philosophers who have not regarded this objection damaging may be supported by what I have said here concerning the confirming power of any evidence which is unopposed.

I shall not, however, continue to press this point: I leave the reader to reach his own conclusion. My major point was to show that empirical evidence, which should be construed as confirming Theism, exists. Thus, if required to summarize briefly the main thesis advanced in this book, I would say: I claim that the traditional theist need not recoil from examining his basic propositions by a method of inquiry which adopts the standards employed in science. On a correct understanding of the essence of scientific method, Theism does not stand to lose from such an inquiry; in fact it gains, emerging from it with enhanced credibility.

INDEX

PHILOSOPHICAL STUDIES SERIES
IN PHILOSOPHY

Editors:

WILFRID SELLARS, Univ. of Pittsburgh and KEITH LEHRER, Univ. of Arizona

Board of Consulting Editors:

Jonathan Bennett, Alan Gibbard, Robert Stalnaker, and Robert G. Turnbull